THE MOST BEAUTIFUL CHINESE MINDS SERIES

“最美中国人”丛书

VOLUNTEERS: MAKING THE WORLD A BETTER PLACE

志愿者：让爱传递到每个角落

“最美中国人”丛书编委会 编著

SinolinguA
华语教学出版社

First Edition 2022

ISBN 978-7-5138-2278-7

Published by Sinolingua Co., Ltd
24 Baiwanzhuang Street, Beijing 100037, China
Tel: (86)10-68320585, 68997826
Fax: (86)10-68997826, 68326333
http://www.sinolingua.com.cn
E-mail: hyjx@sinolingua.com.cn
Facebook: www.facebook.com/sinolingua
Printed by Beijing Hucais Culture Communication Co., Ltd.

Printed in the People's Republic of China

“最美中国人”
丛书编委会

主　编

王君校　韩　晖

张　坤　毛　浩　董　时

编　委

韩　颖　付　眉　刘小琳　张　超

黄　勇　许　革　吴晓东　付豪杰　王荣华

编　务

马博韬

前言

“最美中国人”丛书以中英对照的形式向外国读者讲述新时代中国人民的奋斗故事。本丛书用细致生动的笔触介绍了志愿者、创业者、90后、普通百姓和老年人这几个不同人群中的典型故事，反映出中国人民在中国共产党的领导下实现全面小康的逐梦历程。丛书一共五册，分别是《志愿者：让爱传递到每个角落》《创业者：幸福是奋斗出来的》《出彩90后：我的青春不后悔》《平凡老百姓：把日子过出精气神儿》《中国“传家宝”：那些可爱的老人们》，每册包含八到十个真实故事。为了让外国读者更加直观地了解中国社会的发展和人民生活的巨大变迁，丛书除了文字故事之外，部分故事还配有视频二维码，读者扫描二维码即可观看与文章配套的人物故事视频。

FOREWORD

"The Most Beautiful Chinese Minds" is a book series for international readers featuring stories of Chinese people from all walks of life in today's China. Presented in both Chinese and English, the series reveals the vivid and personal stories of the everyday lives of volunteers, entrepreneurs, post-90s youth, ordinary people and senior citizens as they strive to realize their own dreams and the national dream of building a moderately prosperous society in all aspects under the leadership of the Chinese Communist Party. The series includes five volumes: *Volunteers: Making the World a Better Place*, *Entrepreneurs: Striving for Happiness*, *Born in the 90s: Never Regretting Our Youth*, *Ordinary People: Living a Vibrant Life*, and *Charming Seniors: Keeping Up with the Times.* Each volume consists of eight to ten true stories about real people. It is a must-read for those wishing to better understand the true experiences of everyday Chinese people in today's China and the remarkable changes taking place in their lives. We have also provided QR codes for some stories which can link to online videos about the people from the passages.

目录 | CONTENTS

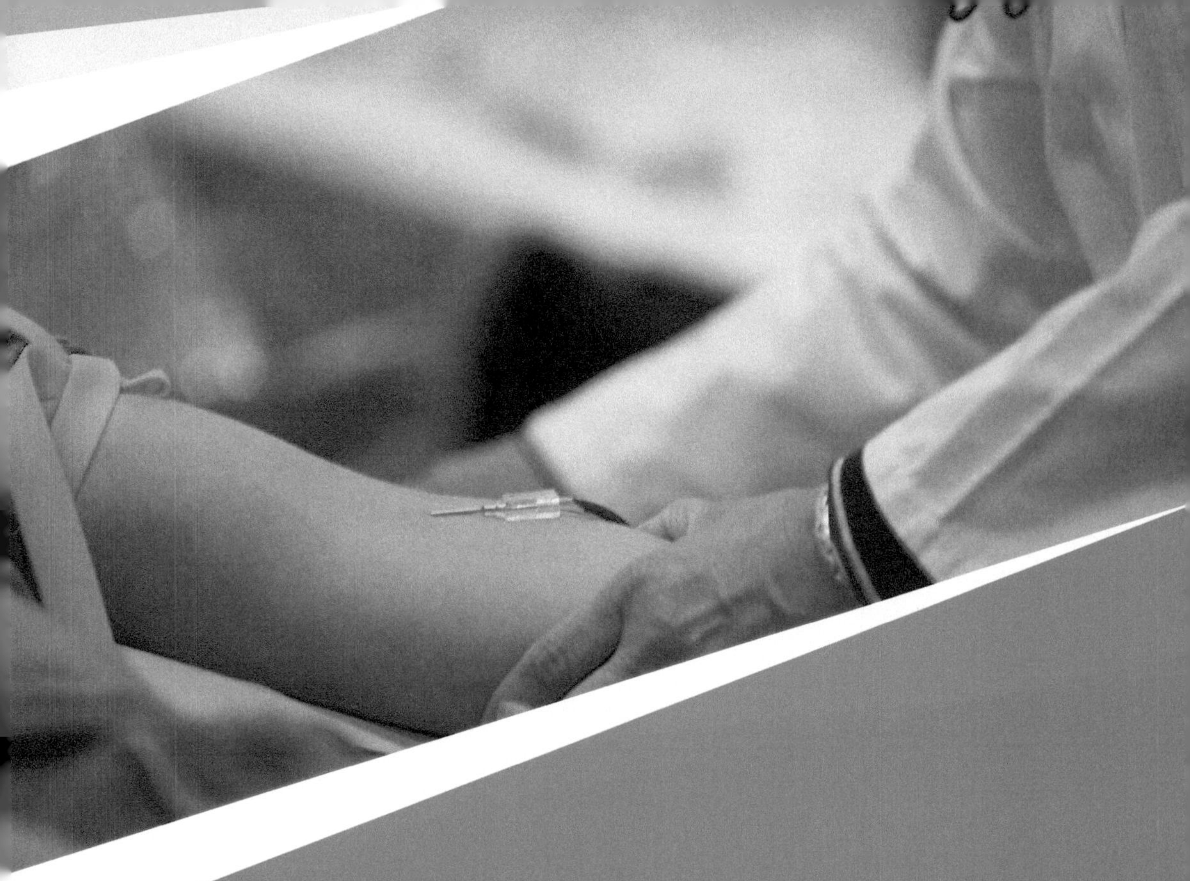

一名 90 后公益人和他的“蓝哈达”

The Blue Khata Charity of a Millennial

作者：张　敏
翻译：李冰青

一名 90 后公益人和他的“蓝哈达”

徐小钢是中国华能金桥热电厂的一名90后员工，但从他的微信朋友圈看不出他是个90后。他发的内容多为寻找走失老人或儿童、流浪动物领养，以及走访留守儿童、看望孤寡老人的信息，鲜有个人生活状态。他的微信个人简介上写着：蓝哈达爱心公益发起人。

“蓝哈达爱心公益协会”是活跃在内蒙古呼和浩特市及周边区域的爱心团队，有近1000名志愿者，成员80%为90后，2015年12月31日在民政局注册成功。自从发起这个组织，徐小钢工作之余的全部生活就是寻找走丢的老人、孩子，救助流浪的猫、狗，帮助路上需要帮助的行人。

当兵的经历让1992年出生的徐小钢身上有股“正义劲儿”，而参加公益活动让他的正义多了几分温暖。2011年，还在部队当兵的徐小钢在广播中听到有孕妇急需B型血，而他正好符合要求，他便请假去献血。

考虑到徐小钢当天还有任务，队长担心他身体吃不消就没有同意。午休时，他辗转反侧，最终冒着被处罚的危险翻墙出去，跑到最近的献血站去献血。他告诉工作人员：“我要把血献给上午广播里说的急需用血的孕妇。”

第一次献爱心让徐小钢觉得自己的生命非常有意义。退伍后，他从广播里听到有孕妇需要血小板，就又一次到献血中心捐献了200毫升的血小板，这一天还是他的生日。这样的爱心之举在徐小钢生活中数不胜数，不论是在上下班的路上还是看到求助信息，只要他能帮得上忙，他都会伸出援手。逐渐地，他想让爱心辐射到更多的人，于是他便召集身边的朋友一起奉献爱心。

2015年接送高考考生是徐小钢第一次有规模地组织集体公益行动。高考前一天，徐小钢突然想到，高考当天会有不少考生出行不便，于是他决定组织车队来接送考生。他在微信朋友圈里说了自己的想法，很快就得到60多个朋友的回复。高考当天，有20多名私家车主参与了活动，一部分车主负责接送已经对接好的考生，一部分车主在路上寻找需要接送的考生。那次他们一共接送了200多位考生。

在呼和浩特，每到高考日时，市交警队就会向有接送考生需求的私家车或爱心出租车免费发放绿丝带并绑在汽车的左反光镜上，以方便载有考生的车辆通行。为示区别，徐小钢和他的伙伴们在右反光镜上绑上了蓝哈达，从此“蓝哈达爱心公益协会”应运而生。对此，“蓝哈达”志愿者乌娅娜解释说：“蒙古民族始终崇拜大自然，无比敬慕天空之蓝，蓝色是纯净的颜色。”

从此，接送高考考生成为“蓝哈达”的固定活动。2016年，他们的接送更加规范、有效。高考前，“蓝哈达”对接了呼和浩特市第二中学的老师，通过学校发布了爱心接送信息，有40多位考生提出了申请。这次接送考生的志愿者中，大部分都是刚工作的90后，还有一位怀孕4个月的孕妇。

高考前一天，志愿者到考生家踩点，计算好到考场的时间，以防高考当天出现差错。上午9点开考，不少志愿者7点就已经等候在考生家门口。送到考点后，这些志愿者聚在一起吃早点，说说各条路的交通情况，等到考试快结束时，他们再回到考点接考生回家。

高考成绩出来后，考生向这些志愿者报告了自己的成绩。“听到他们的成绩不错，我们就觉得很欣慰。”徐小钢说。考试结束后，一些家长还准备了购物卡、礼物想答谢志愿者，但都被他们拒绝了。徐小钢道出了志愿者们的心声：“我们只是想通过公益行为把这种正能量传递给更多人。”

“蓝哈达”就这样被越来越多的人所知道，加入协会的人越来越多。徐小钢的微信好友也从 1000 多人增长到 5000 人，他自己开玩笑地说：“这让我有点恐慌，是不是里面有不少‘僵尸粉’？”

组织志愿者去看望留守儿童、慰问孤寡老人也是“蓝哈达”每个月的固定活动。每次走近这些需要帮助的群体，徐小钢内心最柔软的地方总会被击中。

一次家访贫困学生时，那家的老人不善言语表达，用颤颤巍巍的双手端出了自家种的葡萄表达感谢。徐小钢当过两年兵，即使受伤、受欺负都没让这个身高一米八的小伙子流过一滴泪，而面对老人的这碗葡萄，他竟泪流满面。

2016年的秋天，“蓝哈达”来到呼和浩特托克托县第六中学，又走进了小虎的家里。小虎当时8岁，父亲早逝，母亲跑了，姐弟俩和爷爷奶奶挤在出租屋里，靠捡废品为生。4岁时，小虎得了风湿性关节炎，每个月都需要治疗费，两位老人拉扯着两个孩子艰难地生活着。“蓝哈达”给他们送来了现金、衣物、学习用品。两位老人看着这些年纪不大的志愿者，一句话也说不出，只是不停地流泪。

2017年，徐小钢得知两位老人难以支付小虎每月2000多元的治疗费用后，再一次在朋友圈中组织募捐，并组织志愿者在这一年的最后一天下午到小虎家里送去了捐款和衣物，还带着一家人到饭店吃了顿团圆饭。他说，这是他过得最有意义的一个元旦。

2017年年底，网络上开始流行“佛系青年”的说法。当身边不少朋友将自己归为这一类奉行“看淡一切”“事不关己”态度的群体时，徐小钢认为，年轻人还是应该多为社会奉献一些自己的力量。“如果你身边冷漠的人多，那么你也会被石化，变得麻木，而如果你身边正能量的人多，那你也会被慢慢感化，成为一个温暖的人。在年轻人心里埋下一颗善良的种子，影响的不仅是身边的几个人，更会影响到下一代，影响到整个社会。”

徐小钢和“蓝哈达”所奉献的爱心都是尽己所能，并不是震慑世人的壮举，但却像小火苗一样，在钢筋水泥城市里提供温暖。在徐小钢的带领下，2017 年，“蓝哈达爱心公益协会”被评为第三届“呼和浩特市青年五四奖章集体”，成为 10 个入选集体中唯一的社团组织。拿到这份荣誉，徐小钢非常开心，“说明社会各界对我们很认可”。

徐小钢知道，“蓝哈达”还有很多地方需要完善。目前团队的资金还主要靠爱心企业和志愿者的捐款。每次活动前，他都会在微信群里发布活动信息及财务预算，向志愿者公开募捐，活动结束后，再把明细发到群里接受监督。

“这不是长久的办法，我们要尽快出台更规范严格的规章制度。”徐小钢说，他会一直坚持走下去，“社会需要我们这样的年轻人”。

The Blue Khata Charity of a Millennial

Born in 1992, Xu Xiaogang is a young employee of China Huaneng Jinqiao Cogeneration Power Plant. Unlike his peers who constantly post pictures of their personal lives, his social media is all about looking for missing children and elders, stray animal adoption, visiting left-behind children and the lonely older adults in retirement homes. On his WeChat account, he introduces himself as "the founder of Blue Khata Charity."

The Blue Khata Charity was founded in Hohhot on December 31, 2015. The organization has nearly 1,000 volunteers, and around 80% of them were born in the 90s. Ever since the organization was founded, Xiaogang has spent all of his spare time helping others, such as finding missing elders and children as well as rescuing stray animals.

Xiaogang once served in the military. This experience granted him a sense of justice that extended to helping those in need and contributing to public welfare. In 2011, while he was still a soldier, he heard on the radio that a pregnant woman urgently needed a Type B blood transfusion, and the hospital was calling for Type B blood donors. Luckily, Xiaogang met the requirement. He asked for leave to donate blood. Considering Xiaogang still had training that day and caring about his physical health, his officer did not approve his leave. However, during his lunch break, Xiaogang tossed and turned, thinking about this woman. Later, he finally made his decision. He ran off to the nearest blood donation station, bearing the risk of being punished without having formal leave approval. "I'm going to donate my blood to the pregnant woman who needs blood transfusion broadcast on the radio this morning," he told the nurse in the blood center.

This first experience of helping others made Xiaogang feel his acts are meaningful. After he left the military, Xiaogang went to donate 200ml blood again to a pregnant woman on his birthday. Gradually, Xiaogang developed the habit of helping others. If he could help, he would reach out his hands. Later, Xiaogang decided to gather his friends to offer love and warmth to others.

In 2015, Xiaogang decided to organize free transportation for examinees who had to take the National College Entrance Exam at distant locations. It was the first sizeable charitable activity that Xiaogang had ever organized. He posted his idea on his WeChat Moments and quickly received responses from more than 60 friends. The drivers then contacted the students who needed pick-up services. During the examination, more than 20 private cars were engaged in this free-ride activity. All the drivers drove the students safely to their destinations. There were also some drivers going along the street to see if any other students needed free transportation. During the three days of examination, they drove more than 200 students.

In Hohhot, the traffic police will give green ribbons to private cars and taxis, driving examinees to take the College Entrance Examination. They can tie the ribbons on their left rearview mirror so other cars could see and yield for them. Xiaogang's motorcade uses blue khata and ties it on their right rearview mirror to differentiate them from normal drivers. Ever since this activity, blue khata became the symbol of Xiaogang's charity. Wuyana, a volunteer of Blue Khata Charity, explained, "Mongolians have always worshipped nature. We worship blue since it represents the pure sky. The reason we choose the blue khata as the symbol of our organization is that we will use our purest heart to help others."

Since then, transporting examinees during the National College Entrance Examination has become a regular activity for the Blue Khata Charity. In 2016, their pick-up service became more standardized and effective. Before examination day, Blue Khata contacted teachers in Hohhot No. 2 High School and sent out pick-up information throughout the school. More than 40 students applied for this service that year. Among the volunteers engaging in this free-ride activity, most of them were born in the 90s and just started working, and even a woman who was four-months pregnant participated.

The Blue Khata volunteers are well-prepared for the pick-up service to make sure the students will arrive safely at the test centers. They usually go through a few steps. On the day before the examination, the volunteers will come to the examinees' homes to perform "reconnaissance": volunteers will drive between students' homes and test centers to estimate the time to make sure they won't be late. The exams start at 9 a.m., and usually volunteers will begin waiting outside the students' homes at 7 a.m. After successfully driving students to the centers, the volunteers will gather for breakfast and talk about the traffic conditions of the roads. When the test is almost over, they will drive back to the test center to pick up the examinees.

After the examination results were published, the students would share their results with the volunteers. "We are very pleased to hear about their achievements," Xiaogang said. After the exam, some parents also prepare shopping cards and other gifts to show their gratitude to the volunteers, but volunteers always reject these things. Xiaogang replied, "We just want to pass this positive energy to more people through public welfare activities, and we never think about the return."

Blue Khata was then gradually known by the public. Many people wanted to join the organization. The number of Xiaogang's friends in WeChat also has increased from around 1,000 to 5,000. He jokingly said, "I'm actually kind of in a panic seeing so many people adding me. I even think maybe there are many zombie accounts."

Visiting left-behind children and lonely elders are also regular monthly activities for Blue Khata volunteers. Whenever they see these disadvantaged groups, the softest part of Xu Xiaogang's heart will always be touched.

Once Xiaogang visited a poor student he had funded. The student's grandfather was shy and inarticulate. He offered Xiaogang a full bowl of home grown grapes without saying anything with his trembling hands to express his gratitude. Xiaogang never shed a single tear during the most challenging days in the military. But after seeing this bowl of grapes, this young man's face was covered with tears.

In the autumn of 2016, the Blue Khata volunteers visited Xiaohu, a student in No. 6 Middle School in Togtoh County near Hohhot. Blue Khata started funding Xiaohu since he was eight. At the age of four, Xiaohu was diagnosed with rheumatoid arthritis and had many monthly medical expenses. When Xiaohu turned eight years old, his father passed away, and his mother abandoned him and his sister. His grandparents struggled to raise them. The four of them crowded in a rented place, making a living on picking up waste to cover the family expenses and Xiaohu's medical expenses. After hearing about this situation, Blue Khata brought him money, clothes, and study supplies. Looking at these young volunteers, the grandparents couldn't say a word but kept crying.

In 2017, after hearing the grandparents could no longer afford Xiaohu's monthly medical expenses of 2,000 yuan, Xiaogang organized another fundraiser and sent the donations and clothes to Xiaohu's home on the afternoon of the last day in 2017. He also took Xiaohu's family to a restaurant for a New Year's Eve dinner. "This is the most meaningful New Year's Day I have ever had," Xiaogang recalled.

At the end of 2017, the term "Buddhist-Style Young Man" went viral on the Chinese internet. The phrase showed people's advocacy of settling their minds and calming down their hearts to break off from the fast pace of modern life; however, some people went to an extreme, caring nothing about others and thinking there's nothing to do with themselves. This situation caught Xiaogang's attention, "The younger generation should contribute more to the society. If the people around you are indifferent to others, you will be influenced and become a numb, cold person. If people with positive energy surround you, you will also be influenced and become warm-hearted. Planting a seed of kindness in young people's hearts will not only change people around them but can also be passed out to the next generations, making the world a better place."

What Xiaogang and his Blue Khata Charity have done are minor and normal things. They didn't accomplish big feats, but everything they did was just like a small fire that lit up the city and warmed people's hearts. Under Xiaogang's leadership, the Blue Khata Charity was the only non-profit organization awarded the May Fourth Medal for Outstanding Youth Group of Hohhot in 2017. Xiaogang was very happy to receive the highest honor for youths. He said, "This means society recognizes what we have done."

Xiaogang knows that the organization still needs to make improvements. Blue Khata mainly relies on donations from enterprises and volunteers. Before every activity, Xiaogang will post the fundraising information, financial budget, donation procedures, and donation inventory in group chat, assuring the fund management is subject to supervision.

"Our organization still needs to come out with more standardized and strict regulations for better management," Xiaogang said. "No matter how hard it will be, I will keep running the Blue Khata Charity. Our society needs young volunteers like us."

让法治的阳光照亮雪域高原

Legal Aid in Xizang (Tibet)

作者：王海涵 王 磊 钟欣欣 尤 宽
翻译：李冰青

让法治的阳光照亮雪域高原

工作之余，安徽援藏女律师陈贤经常拿出手机，翻阅在西藏、内蒙古、新疆等地从事法律援助时拍下的照片。照片里有当地纯净优美的自然风光，也有少数民族同胞淳朴善良的笑脸。

每一张照片她都舍不得删掉，这些照片不仅记录了她5年多法律援助工作的点点滴滴，也承载了她和当地群众的深情及她对祖国边疆的无限眷恋。

陈贤是安徽省首位援藏女律师。5年多来，她行走在祖国边疆，为当地群众送去他们急需的法律援助。她热心公益，不仅收获了精神的升华，也收获了边疆群众的信赖和支持。

她经常说："做法律援助工作，让我有机会用专长为国家、为人民尽一份责任，我觉得，此生无憾！"

2019年，陈贤再次主动请缨。7月底，

她前往新疆，开始了自己第6年的法律援助工作。

提前适应高原气候，骑行青海湖

“我甘愿放弃优裕舒适的生活，甘愿忍受亲人离别，甘愿忍受艰苦恶劣的工作和生活环境，顽强拼搏，无私奉献，让法治的阳光照亮雪域高原的每一个角落。”这是陈贤2014年第一次报名参加“1+1”中国法律援助志愿行动时在申请书里写下的一段话。

陈贤之所以对公益行动怀有如此热烈的情感，源于20多年前在她心中埋下的感恩的种子。高二那年，陈贤的父亲因病去世，母亲微薄的工资成为家里仅有的收入。班主任老师了解到她家里的情况后，发动学校师生为她捐款献爱心。“有同学把饭钱全都捐出来，这些细节我至今难忘。”陈贤回忆，自己当时就想将来有条件、有能力了，一定要竭尽所能帮助别人。

2013年的一个夜晚，陈贤无意中在网

上看到失去双手的“1+1”志愿律师郭二玲的事迹，感动不已。

“身残志坚，要克服多少常人难以想象的困难才能成为一名律师，又是怎样的无私大爱才愿意投身公益，扶贫济弱！”陈贤彻夜未眠，她在网上查找相关信息，详细了解“1+1”法律援助志愿行动的报名条件。

当时，陈贤已经错过了当年的报名时间。不甘心放弃的她开始为来年再报名做准备。“为让身体适应高原气候，我和儿子一起去海拔3000多米的青海湖环湖骑行，一天骑行100多公里。”陈贤介绍道。

2014年春天，在家人支持下，陈贤报名成功，最终把服务地定在了西藏。虽然提前做过身体适应，但是高原气候还是给陈贤来了一个“下马威”。

陈贤的援助地是西藏自治区昌都市卡若区，那里平均海拔3500多米。“由于高寒缺氧，那会儿鼻子时常出血。”陈贤说，她皮肤还过敏，痒得很，经常被抓破。

陈贤住在10楼，办公室在4楼，因为

经常停电，她常常得走楼梯。尽管条件艰苦，但陈贤从没有向家人和同事抱怨过，都是“报喜不报忧”。

“比起工作，这些算得了什么呢？多想想工作的获得感、自己的责任。”陈贤没有向困难低头，她积极适应，满腔热情地投入到法律服务工作中。

她去之前，那里没有一名律师

卡若区地处藏东，经济相对发达，开工项目较多，农民工讨薪、工伤案件经常发生。“在我去之前，那里没有一名律师，法律服务资源很薄弱。”陈贤介绍，自己办理的第一个法律援助案件是一起工伤赔偿案。

藏族姑娘扎西曲珍因工伤造成八级伤残，医药费花了几万元，与当事公司在保险待遇上调解不成，起诉到法院。从取证到提供辩护，经过一审、二审、重审，在陈贤的不懈努力下，扎西曲珍拿到了近17万元的工伤保险款。之后，扎西曲珍和舅舅为这位陌生而亲切的汉族法律援助律师送来了一面锦旗。

那一刻，陈贤很感动，“身体再不舒服、环境再恶劣，也是值得的”。

还有一起藏族小伙讨薪案，更加坚定了陈贤投身边疆开展志愿法律援助的决心。藏族农民工次里巨丁起初对陈贤的援助充满怀疑，直到最终拿到判决书、看到法院判决老板偿付所欠的7000多元工资时，次里巨丁才满意地笑了。

“用法律帮助藏族同胞维护权益，加深他们对法律的认知，对我而言就是最大的成就。”陈贤说。

陈贤与司法局同事多次克服艰险路况，下乡发放法律法规宣传资料和自己的名片，解答群众咨询。陈贤说：“我要用办理的每一起案件，告诉少数民族兄弟姐妹，法律面前只有公平正义。”

在西藏开展法律援助的一年时间里，陈贤办结58件案件，为受援群众挽回直接经济损失100多万元。受援群众说，陈贤在他们心里就像格桑花一样美丽。

一年的援助期转眼间到了，2015年，

陈贤申请继续留在西藏开展法律援助工作。组织上考虑她的身体状况，把陈贤派往内蒙古开展法律援助。

在内蒙古服务期间，陈贤曾在零下20摄氏度左右的极寒天气里到乡下露天开展法制宣传，一站就是几个小时，手脚被冻僵。她也曾顶着刺骨的寒风骑着自行车去开庭，开完庭，大雪封路，只能艰难地推着自行车回住处。

陈贤说，每当看到那些绝望无助的当事人因她提供的法律帮助而维权成功，她都觉得自己特别幸福。

伉俪情深，并肩而行

在内蒙古，有一个“惊喜”在等待着陈贤。她的丈夫曹旭律师也申请并获批参加当年“1+1”中国法律援助志愿者行动，援助地也在内蒙古。

陈贤援藏的一年里，她每次和曹旭通电话都成了法律援助成果汇报。曹旭从妻子疲惫但不失兴奋的语调中感受到了奉献的快乐。他一边心疼妻子，一边也意识到法律援助工作的价值所在。

于是，受到感召的曹旭毅然决定，同妻子一起到祖国最需要的地方去！他们也是“1+1”中国法律援助志愿者行动开展以来，全国唯一一对参与法律援助志愿活动的律师夫妻。

虽说和爱人一起来到内蒙古，但是陈贤在巴彦淖尔市乌拉特中旗，曹旭在乌海市海南区，相隔300多公里。陈贤回忆道：“我们俩要见上一面，得转4次车，大概7个小时的车程。”为了不耽误工作，两人往往还没来得及说上几句贴心话，又得匆匆返回。

有时遇到大雪封路，两人很长时间也见不上一面。他们只能约定每天工作结束后打电话报平安。在那种环境下，每天的通话成了夫妻俩消除疲劳的最好方式。

工作中，陈贤与曹旭互帮互助，生活中，他们也是一对令人称羡的恩爱伴侣，两人不仅有说不完的话，还常常一起运动、旅行。

“其实，我能有今天的成绩，和丈夫的

支持与鼓励密不可分。”据陈贤介绍，曹旭的父亲是一名老法律工作者，弟弟妹妹现在也都从事法律相关职业。

在曹旭的影响下，陈贤自学法律，并顺利通过了国家司法考试，成为一名律师。后来陈贤又影响了曹旭，夫妻俩一起在志愿律师这条征途上并肩而行。

2016 年到 2018 年，陈贤又被派到新疆乌鲁木齐市头屯河区开展志愿法律援助工作。

“日子苦、条件差、挣不到钱，去那里干啥？”陈贤的儿子曹天楚大学毕业后通过了国家司法考试。起初，他并不理解母亲为何要去边疆做志愿服务。

2017 年，陈贤一家三口难得团聚，在新疆过春节。“看到那么多需要帮助的农民工在讨薪维权，母亲为他们伸张正义，还有那么多群众发自内心地拥护和信赖母亲时，我被真正打动了，意识到母亲在做一件多么伟大的事。将来，我也要和父母一样，成为一名真心为民、服务基层群众的好律师。”曹天楚感慨道。

2018年，曹天楚成为了一名实习律师，在家乡工作，实习期满后，他将成为正式律师。“这是儿子自己的选择，我和他爸都很欣慰，很开心。”陈贤说，自己要继续努力，争取给儿子做个好榜样。

Legal Aid in Xizang (Tibet)

Ms. Chen Xian is a lawyer working in Xizang. During her spare time, she often takes out her phone and looks through her photos. They are of the beautiful natural scenes of Xizang, Inner Mongolia and Xinjiang autonomous regions, and the beautiful smiles of the ethnic minority people she has helped there.

She does not want to delete a single picture. These photos are a record of her five years of legal aid there, and also of her infinite affection for the borderlands and local people.

Chen Xian is the first lawyer in Anhui Province to join the 1+1 China Voluntary Legal Aid Program and start legal aid in Xizang. She is enthusiastic about public welfare. Over the past five years, she has helped people in the borderlands deal with various urgent legal issues. The experience has been very spiritual for her, and it has helped her win the trust and love of the local people.

"Devoting myself to legal aid work has given me the chance to utilize what I have learned to help the people of my country and realize my responsibility as a lawyer. As a result, I don't have any regrets in my life," she said.

In 2019, Chen Xian signed up again for the 1+1 China Voluntary Legal Aid Program, and she was assigned to work in Xinjiang Uygur

Autonomous Region. At the end of July, she left for Xinjiang, starting her sixth year of legal assistance.

Preparing for the Plateau Climate

"I'm willing to give up my comfortable life and endure the hardship of separating from my family and working on the Xizang Plateau in order to devote myself to legal assistance, utilizing the power of law to light up every corner of the plateau." This was what Chen Xian wrote in her first 1+1 China Voluntary Legal Aid Program application in 2014.

The reason why Chen has such a strong interest in public welfare can be traced back 20 years. While she was in 11th grade, her father passed away, and her mother's meager salary became the family's only income. After learning of their situation, the teacher in charge of Chen Xian's class organized a donation in her high school. As a result, many teachers and students donated portions of their salaries and lunch money to help her family. "I'll never forget their kindness. It was then that I made up my mind to do my best to help others if I'm capable, to pass out the kindness I received to others who also need it."

One night in 2013, Chen stumbled upon the story of Guo Erling, a disabled volunteer lawyer who lost both of her hands, and was greatly touched by the story.

"With a physical impairment, Erling overcame numerous obstacles to become a lawyer. But instead of pursuing high salaries, she devoted herself to helping the poor!" she recalled. Chen spent a sleepless night searching online for information about 1+1 China Voluntary Legal Aid Program.

At that time, she had already missed the application deadline for that year. She started to prepare for the following year. "I started exercising with my son, riding about 100 km a day around Qinghai Lake at an attitude of over 3,000 meters to physically adapt to the plateau climate."

In spring 2014, with the support of her family, she successfully became a lawyer who was assigned to work in Xizang. Although she had exercised in advance, she was still not totally prepared for the plateau climate.

She went to work in Karub District, Qamdo where the average altitude is above 3,500 meters. "Because of the plateau coldness and hypoxia, my nose was always bleeding." She also had skin allergies and often felt itchy, so she was often scratching.

She lived on the tenth floor, and the office was on the fourth floor. Because of the frequent power outages, she often had to take the stairs. Despite these challenging conditions, she never complained to her family or colleagues. She only shared positive things with them and never said anything about the hardships she endured.

"The satisfaction of completing a case and the responsibility of being a lawyer offset those hardships." She did not buckle under the difficulties. Instead, she enthusiastically devoted herself to her legal work.

The First Lawyer

Karub district is located in eastern Xizang with a relatively developed economy and many ongoing infrastructure construction projects, but the area still lacks legal resources. As a result, cases involving unpaid wages and work-related injury compensation happen a lot. "Before I arrived there, the district didn't have any lawyers, and legal services were scarce," Chen Xian stated. "My very first legal aid case here was related to work injury compensation."

Tashi Chodron, a local woman, was injured at work and reached level 8 disability after the injury. She spent tens of thousands of yuan on medical treatment and could not reconcile insurance compensation with her company, so she sued them. Chen Xian acted as her lawyer and collected evidence. The case went through the first trial, a second trial, and even a retrial. In the end, Tashi received about 170,000 yuan in compensation. After that, Tashi and her uncle sent Chen a banner to show their gratitude to this unfamiliar yet cordial lawyer.

When Chen saw the banner, she was moved. "No matter how bad I felt physically or how challenging the environment is, that made it all worth it."

There was also the case of a young man named Cili Juding who hadn't received his wages. When she first met him, he did not trust her and did not believe she could help him. Only after he received the final verdict and 7,000 yuan of salary did he finally smile at Chen with satisfaction.

"People here have little understanding of the law, which means they can't use the law as a weapon to protect their rights. Helping them learn about the law and deepen their understanding of the rule of law is the best thing I could ever do," Chen Xian said.

Chen and officials of the local judicial bureau had to overcome challenging road conditions to visit villagers who lived in remote areas on the plateau in order to teach them about basic knowledge of the law. "I wanted to tell my ethnic minority brothers and sisters that the law is always fair, and the law can solve any injustice they experience."

In just one year, Chen completed 58 cases, helping her clients avoid more than 1 million yuan of direct economic losses. The clients praised her, saying that in their hearts, she was as beautiful as a galsang flower.

After that first year, she applied to continue her term of service. But because of her physical condition, the program director assigned her to Inner Mongolia. That was 2015.

Working in Inner Mongolia was also not easy. Chen once held an open-air legal seminar in the countryside, standing outside for several hours in -20°C weather. After the seminar her hands and feet were frozen. Sometimes she had to ride to the courthouse in the bitter cold on a bicycle. After her case was over, the road was blocked by heavy snow, so she had to push her bicycle all the way back to her residence.

But when she wins the cases, and sees the desperate people she helps fight for their rights and succeed, she feels happy.

Wife and Husband

In Inner Mongolia, a "surprise" was waiting for Chen Xian. Her husband Cao Xu, also a lawyer, had just been approved to join the legal aid program and had also been sent to Inner Mongolia.

During the previous year when Chen Xian worked in Xizang, her phone calls to Cao Xu were always about her cases. He could feel the joy and dedication through his wife's tired but excited tone over the phone. Though he was concerned about her health, he gradually came to understand the deep value of legal aid work.

Because of her, he decided to also join the legal aid service. Since the 1+1 China Legal Aid Program was launched, they are the only lawyer couple to have participated in the program.

Although they were both in Inner Mongolia, they were unfortunately not assigned to the same city. Chen Xian worked in Urad Middle Banner, Bayannur City while Cao Xu worked in Hainan District, Wuhai City, which was about 300 kilometers away. "When we wanted to meet, we needed to spend 7 hours on the bus and transfer four times," Chen Xian recalled. "We didn't have much time to spend together. We could only be together for a short while and then had to return in a hurry."

Sometimes during the winter, heavy snow blocked the roads, and they could not see each other for long periods of time. The couple agreed to call each other every day after they finished work. Their daily conversations helped them relieve fatigue, and give support to one another.

At work, they supported each other. In their personal lives, their marriage is wonderful. The couple exercises and travels together, sharing everything with each other.

"I could not have made all my achievements without my husband's support and encouragement," Chen Xian said happily. She said that her father-in-law was also an experienced lawyer, and her husband's younger brothers and sisters also had careers related to the law.

It was because of Cao Xu that Chen Xian studied law and became a lawyer. Later, it was Chen Xian who influenced Cao Xu to become a volunteer lawyer. The couple has been on this journey together now for many years.

In 2016, Chen Xian was sent to Urumqi in Xinjiang to provide local legal aid services.

"The days are hard, the conditions are poor and you can't make money. Why go there?" Chen Xian's son, Cao Tianchu, who passed the national judicial examination after graduation, couldn't understand why his mother chose to be a volunteer lawyer.

In 2017, the family finally reunited and spent the Spring Festival together in Xinjiang. This was when her son began to see things differently. "I saw so many migrant workers needing help to retrieve unpaid wages, I saw my mother defending their rights, and I saw how they supported and trusted her. This really moved me. I finally realized the significance of my mother's career. That was when I decided that I also wanted to become a good lawyer who truly serves people like my parents," Cao Tianchu recalled emotionally.

In 2018, Cao Tianchu became an intern lawyer and worked in his hometown. After he passes the internship, he will become an official lawyer. "This is my son's choice. We are very happy to see him choose this path," Chen Xian said. She said she will continue working hard to set a good example for her son.

警察和小熊

The Policeman and the Bear

作者：张　渺
翻译：韩芙芸

警察和小熊

林敏明脱下警服，就变成了“雄熊叔叔”。

他是福建省司法警察训练总队的一名教官，从警近20年。福建各个监狱的民警如果到总队培训，都可能会成为他的学员。林敏明对参训学员要求严格，学员们都叫他林老师、林队。

林敏明同时是福建省教育援助协会的发起人之一。协会还有个名字叫“红苹果公益”，协会统一制作的衣服上印着一只带着笑脸的红苹果，“就像孩子红扑扑的小脸”。他们专门给服刑人员等特殊家庭的未成年子女提供教育、心理、法律等层面的援助。

有的孩子因为小时候见过警察把手铐铐在亲人手腕上，所以长大后一见到制服、警徽、警车就浑身发抖。林敏明把一只蓝灰色的小熊玩偶挂在协会工作服上。他问孩子：“雄熊叔叔也是警察，你会怕吗？”

他听孩子们讲学校的事，跟他们聊动画片，也会给他们带印着卡通图案的书包和玩具。那些孩子都喜欢林敏明，叫他“雄熊叔叔”。

2014年6月，“红苹果公益”正式注册成立，迄今已经建立了12个监狱教育援助中心，登记的志愿者800多名，其中将近70%的志愿者都是警察。

这些监狱民警审核过家属和服刑人员的通信。一位曾经遭受丈夫家庭暴力并最终杀死了丈夫的女犯人收到了儿子的来信，被亲戚抚养的儿子在信里告诉母亲，自己考上了大学，学法律专业，“这所学校您可能不知道”。那是一所北京的211重点大学，就连审核信件的民警林苏都感慨，“这学校太难考了”。林苏猜测，这个男孩选择学法律“也许是因为父母的事情”。

但更多时候，监狱民警看到的信件没有那么鼓舞人心。许多服刑人员的子女也成了监狱的常客，彼此之间寄信“交流坐牢的心得”，讨论刑期和怎样“获得加分”。

一位女犯平时表现很好，改造积极，很

少流泪。她哭的那几次都是因为收到了孩子的信。那是一个父母双服刑的家庭，她和丈夫坐牢之后，两个儿子陆续也进了监狱，一个因为抢劫，另一个因为参与了群体打架斗殴。

司法部曾在2005年开展“监狱服刑人员未成年子女基本问题”调研工作。统计数据显示，中国服刑人员未成年子女总数超过60万，其中九成以上没有得到过任何形式的社会救助。在中国未成年人罪犯的总数里，服刑人员子女占了一半。

2017年7月，“红苹果公益”对福建省18所监狱中，有未成年子女的在押服刑人员进行了摸底调查。这些人平均家中有一两个孩子，加在一起共计17922个孩子。这些孩子的辍学率达26.9%，三成有心理问题，超过五分之一存在触犯法律的行为。

“红苹果公益”成立前，不止一位监狱民警向林敏明提起过服刑人员子女的境遇。2012年的一个夜晚，一群正在警察训练总队培训的监狱民警把林敏明围在中间，你一言我一语，讨论着对服刑人员子女进行帮扶的可行性。那时，林敏明已经参与公益活动3年多，累计参加志愿服务的小时数已经上千。

“我被大家‘架’起来了。”林敏明回忆道，“但回去以后，由于大家工作任务繁重，渐渐把这件事淡忘了，我就牵头把事情做了。”

一年时间里，林敏明利用周末跋涉了两万公里，拜访了100多户人家，入户探访时忙到没时间吃饭。他和志愿者一起与服刑人员家属沟通，与孩子谈心。

第一次走访是在2013年年底。那时林敏明和整个团队都没经验。车子开进村子，志愿者摇下车窗，打听那户人家的住处。

“去这家干吗呀？他们家的媳妇杀人啦！”村民不愿意指路。

林敏明没法子，只好去了那户人家的孩子就读的学校，找到孩子的老师，证明了自己身份，这才找到了那户人家。

那时候，“红苹果公益”没什么知名度，孩子的爷爷根本不信任林敏明，把他当成了人贩子。那次走访结束之后还有人打来电话，追问、确认他的身份。

很多孩子都会被家人重点保护起来。柳茵（化名）和丈夫因为经济案件入狱时，女儿6岁。小女孩儿进进出出永远有亲戚陪着，很少见陌生人，家里人怕她“听到闲话”。她变得比同龄人成熟和沉默，很少大哭大笑。

柳茵前年出狱了，但丈夫判的是无期徒刑，一家人的团聚遥遥无期。女儿问她：“你们不知道父亲做的事是错的吗？当初为什么没人拉住他？”柳茵无言以对。

“如果当时有人告诉我欠钱不还是要坐牢的，我一定不会这样做。”她对记者说。她16岁出来打拼，自幼居住的小山村几乎没多少人家，没什么人会告诉她，除了杀人放火，还有哪些事也是犯罪。

林敏明打开“红苹果公益”数据库收集的信息，许多服刑人员提交的愿望里，都写的是希望给孩子提供“普法”和“心理”援助。

“给这些孩子提供心理辅导和法律援助，不但能促进孩子身心健康，也能促进社会治理与建设。”林敏明说。“红苹果公益”

成立了一个专家指导委员会，细分为心理帮扶组、社会工作组和法律援助组。林敏明聘来10多名心理咨询师志愿者，以及儿童心理学、认知心理学等专业的导师，给志愿者进行培训。

据林敏明描述，许多服刑人员家庭生活在贫困线以下。但是村、县往往“戴着有色眼镜”，不愿意把这样的家庭列在困难名单里。“农村根深蒂固的思想，认为龙生龙，凤生凤，老鼠的儿子会打洞。”

林敏明记得有一个家庭：妻子曾因产后抑郁自焚，结果烧毁了屋子，自己也深度烧伤，成了残疾人；丈夫开黑车谋生，因抢客源与人斗殴入狱，这个家庭原本就因医药费背着十几万元的外债，丈夫入狱又失去了经济来源，3个孩子最大的在上高中，最小的还在幼儿园。还有一个家庭：丈夫入狱，患有脑瘤和腿疾的妻子，苦苦支撑，有时儿子在学校表现不好被请家长，她忍不住会把压力发泄到孩子身上，她时刻担心自己的身体要是撑不下去了，儿子又该怎么办。

为这些家庭争取经济补助，也成了林敏

明的工作之一。

“我们在狱中开展‘穿墙引线’、亲情拓展营等活动，联系司法部门帮服刑人员的孩子解决各种问题，协调民政机构帮这些家庭申请低保救助的‘兜底’工作，请教育部门陪伴教育孩子，联络共青团‘入户探访’……”林敏明一个一个地数着。

这些事情，他用警察的身份没有办法做到。他开始“撕掉标签”，“不用名字”，于是警察林敏明变成了“雄熊叔叔”。

“雄熊叔叔”和“红苹果公益”为这些孩子筹集善款，结对捐助，在福建省的10多所监狱举办了亲情拓展营活动。与每月一次、隔着玻璃的常规亲属会见不同，在“红苹果”的亲情拓展营里，服刑人员可以抱起自己的孩子，亲亲他们的小脸。

用福清监狱监狱长林明飞的话说，对服刑者日常管理，“约谈100次的效果，都不如让他参加一次‘红苹果’的亲情拓展营”。

刚过去的这个假期，在漳州监狱教育援助中心和共青团漳州市委共同举办的父亲节、端午节活动中，一位父亲在入狱将近3

年后第一次见到女儿。他被捕时，女儿刚学会走路，小小的人儿总爱跟着爸爸。如今，小女孩儿看着眼前陌生的脸，把头埋进妈妈怀里，谁来哄都不理。父亲坐在旁边，眼泪一颗一颗地落下。

截至2017年12月，“红苹果公益”共援助3360多人次，服刑人员未成年子女帮扶覆盖至中国的322个县市，挽救了辍学儿童35人。到目前为止，在册帮扶的1473个未成年人当中，没有发生辍学和犯罪的现象；帮扶后出狱的140多个服刑人员没有任何一个再次犯罪。

也有林敏明觉得遗憾的例子：一个男孩已经十六七岁了，父亲在服刑。志愿者几次上门都没能见到孩子本人。后来林敏明听说，那个孩子也违法入狱了，而且是“二进宫”“三进宫”。

“如果我们能在他犯错误之前见到他，给他提供帮助和疏导，也许就不是这个结果了。”林敏明说。

逢年过节，都会有小礼物送到孩子手中。许多孩子回信说，这是他们第一次收到礼物。林敏明“无法想象”会有这么多小孩儿从没有得到过礼物。他的办公室里，来自服刑人员、家属和孩子的信件被装在档案夹里，搁了满满一柜子。

在信中，有的孩子倾诉被同学欺负的经历，他哭着回家想要找爸爸反而被妈妈训斥；有的孩子担忧外公外婆的身体，想快快长大，帮忙分担；有的孩子喜欢唱歌，在来信中倾诉想成为歌唱家的愿望，但“家里没钱，我的梦想可能没有了”。

“我要是能帮到他们更多一点就好了。”林敏明常常这样感慨。

他曾前往哈佛大学和麻省理工学院参加高级公益慈善领导人培训课程，见到了很多国外的公益人士。他问他们国外有没有类似“红苹果公益”这样的机构，对方说不了解。

林敏明自己在网上查，查到美国有一些类似的小公益机构，帮扶面较小，大多只是提供心理辅导之类的援助。他猜是由于国情不同，需求也有所不同。在服刑人员未成年子女帮扶的事情上，他找不到太多可供参考的例子了。有时候他会觉得，自己像是“摸着石头过河”，每一步踏出去，都不知前路如何。

“红苹果公益”的资金仍然捉襟见肘，需要帮扶的孩子有2000多个，每人每年补贴1000—3000元，对这些家庭来说只是杯水车薪。

但林敏明对未来很有信心，这个群体正在被越来越多的人关注。他希望“红苹果模式”能推广到全中国，让更多的孩子受益。

The Policeman and the Bear

Lin Minming takes off his police uniform, changes into his plain clothes and becomes "Uncle Bear."

He is an instructor at the Fujian Provincial Judicial Police Training Corps and has been a police officer for nearly 20 years. He specializes in training police officers stationed at prisons in Fujian Province. Lin is strict with his trainees, and they all respectfully call him Teacher Lin or Captain Lin.

He is also one of the founders of the Fujian Provincial Education Assistance Association, also named "Red Apple Public Welfare." Its uniform features a red apple with a smiley face, "just like a child's red face," he says. The association provides educational, psychological, legal, and other assistance to minors from families of prisoners.

Some children may shudder at the sight of uniforms, badges, and police cars because they saw people they love in handcuffs when they were young. Lin has a small toy bear doll hanging on his work clothes. He often points to it and asks children, "Uncle Bear is also a policeman. Are you still afraid?"

He listens to their stories about school, talks with them about cartoons, and brings them bags and toys with cartoon pictures on them. The children all like Lin Minming and call him Uncle Bear.

In June 2014, Red Apple Public Welfare was officially registered. So far, it has set up 12 centers for prison education assistance, and more than 800 volunteers are available for help, nearly 70% of whom are police officers.

Prison police officers will examine the correspondence between family members and inmates. A woman who was the victim of domestic violence and eventually killed her husband received a letter from her son. The son, raised by a relative, told his mother that he had gone to college to study law at "a university you may not know." It actually was one of the Project 211 key universities in Beijing. Even Lin Su, the police officer who examined the letter, said, "It is very hard to enter that university." Lin Su speculated that the boy had chosen to study law "perhaps because things happened between his parents."

But more often than not, letters they read are less encouraging. Many of the inmates' children have also become prison regulars, writing letters to each other to "exchange experiences of imprisonment," discuss jail terms and how to "earn points."

There was one particular female prisoner who usually behaved well, acted positively, and rarely shed tears. The few times she cried were after she had received letters from her children. After she and her husband went to prison, their two sons also ended up in prison, one for robbery and the other for being involved in a group fight.

In 2005, the Ministry of Justice of China conducted a survey on "Basic Questions for Minor Children of Prisoners." Statistics showed that China had more than 600,000 underage children of prisoners, of whom more than 90% had not received any form of social assistance.

Children of prisoners accounted for half of the total number of juvenile offenders in China.

In July 2017, Red Apple Public Welfare conducted a thorough survey of inmates of 18 prisons in Fujian Province with such children. On average, these inmates had one or two children at home, totaling 17,922 children. The school dropout rate for these children was 26.9%. 30% of them had psychological problems, and more than one-fifth had broken the law.

Before establishing Red Apple Public Welfare, some prison police officers mentioned to Lin Minming the situation of the prisoners' children. One night in 2012, a group of prison police officers training in the corps spoke with Lin about the feasibility of helping these children. At that time, Lin had been involved in public welfare activities for more than three years, accumulating over one thousand hours of volunteer activity participation.

"They all expected I could do something to help." Lin recalls, "But when they went back to work, they gradually forgot about the idea because they were so busy. But I didn't forget. I took the lead in getting it done."

In one year, Lin traveled some 20,000 kilometers over the weekends to visit more than 100 families; sometimes, he was even too busy to eat. Together with volunteers, he spoke with the family members about the inmates and talked to their children.

His first visit was at the end of 2013. At that time, Lin and his team had no experience. They were looking for a particular family. They drove into the village, and a volunteer rolled down the window to ask directions to the family.

"Why do you want to see this family?" a local resident asked. "Their daughter-in-law killed someone!"

Lin had no choice but to go to the children's school to find the teacher. After he showed his identity, they were finally taken to the family.

At that time, Red Apple Public Welfare was not well known, so the child's grandfather did not trust them and even thought Lin might be a human trafficker. After the visit, someone even called to confirm his identity.

The families tended to overprotect these children. Liu Yin (pseudonym) and her husband were jailed for economic crimes when their daughter was six years old. The little girl was always accompanied by relatives when she got out, and she was not allowed to speak to strangers as the family was afraid that she might "hear gossip." She grew up to be more mature than her peers, was often quiet, and rarely cried or laughed.

Liu Yin was released from prison, but her husband was serving a life sentence. One day her daughter asked her, "Didn't you know what father did was wrong? Why didn't anyone stop him?" Liu Yin was speechless.

"If I'd been told that I would go to jail if I didn't pay my debts, I never would have done it," she said. She had come out to work at the age of 16 from a small mountain village. She had lived there since childhood, and there were few people. No one had ever told her that besides murder and arson, there were other crimes, too.

Lin Minming accessed the information database collected by Red Apple Public Welfare to show that many prisoners had submitted their wish that their children be provided with legal and psychological assistance.

"Providing psychological counseling and legal assistance to these children can not only benefit their physical and mental health, but can also positively impact social governance and construction," Lin said. Red Apple Public Welfare has set up an expert committee which is divided into groups specializing in psychological support, social work and legal aid. Lin has invited more than ten volunteer counselors and professional mentors on children's psychology, cognitive psychology and other specific disciplines to train volunteers.

According to Lin Minming, many families of the prisoners live below the poverty line. But villages and counties are often biased, and are reluctant to put such families on the list of poor families. "The deep-rooted idea in the countryside is 'like father, like son.'"

Lin mentioned one family in which a new mother experienced postpartum depression and set fire to herself, which caused the house to burn. She survived, but got deep burns and became disabled. To earn money, her husband drove an illegal taxi. He was thrown into prison for fighting with competitors for customers. The family had previously accrued hundreds of thousands of yuan in debt for medical expenses. When the husband went to prison, the family lost financial support. They had three children; the oldest was in high school, and the youngest was still in kindergarten.

Another story entailed a family in which the wife suffered from a brain tumor and leg disease, but once her husband was jailed, she had to support the family alone. Her son often performed badly in school, and she would yell at him. She constantly worried what would happen to him if her health worsened.

Securing financial aid for these families has also become one of Lin's jobs.

"We've carried out activities such as a family relationship development camp called Thread Through the Wall, which helps connect prisoners with their family; have contacted the judiciary to help children of prisoners solve various problems; have coordinated civil affairs to help these families apply for basic living allowances; have invited the education department to accompany and educate the children; and have contacted the Communist Youth League to do home visits..."

Lin said that since he could not do these things as a policeman, he "tore off the label and did not use his name." That's when he became "Uncle Bear."

Uncle Bear and Red Apple Public Welfare raised money for the children, set up pairing donations, and held family development camps in more than ten prisons in Fujian Province. Unlike regular monthly meetings through glass barriers, inmates can pick up their children and kiss their little faces in the Red Apple camp.

Fuqing Prison warden Lin Mingfei said, "The effect of 100 visits is not as good as letting prisoners participate in one Red Apple family development camp."

For the holidays of Father's Day and the Dragon Boat Festival, the Zhangzhou Prison Education Assistance Center and the Communist Youth League Zhangzhou Municipal Committee jointly organized a celebration. A father in prison saw his daughter for the first time in nearly three years. Before he was arrested, his daughter had just learned to walk, and the little girl had always loved to walk behind her father, following him. Now, she looked at the strange face in front of her, buried her head into her mother's arms, and ignored everyone. Her father sat next to her in tears.

As of December 2017, Red Apple had assisted more than 3,360 people, including minor children of prisoners in 322 counties and cities in China, of whom 35 had dropped out of school and had subsequently been brought back to school with the help of Red Apple. To date, of the 1,473 minors registered for assistance, there have been no school drop-outs or crimes. Of the more than 140 released inmates whose children have been helped, none have re-committed crimes.

There are some stories that Lin Minming regrets, such as a boy of 16 or 17 years old whose father is serving a prison sentence. Many times, the volunteers failed to see him. Later, Lin heard that the child was also jailed, and has been incarcerated three times now.

"If we could have seen him before he made his mistake, and given him help and guidance, maybe this would not be the result," Lin said.

On New Year's Day or other holidays, Red Apple will send small gifts to the children. Many children have written back that it was the first time they had ever received a gift. Lin finds it hard to imagine that so many children have never been given gifts. In his office are letters from inmates, their family members and children, all packed in files, filling the whole cabinet.

In one letter, a child confided the experience of being bullied by classmates. He cried while walking home, and wanted to look for his father but was scolded by his mother. In another letter, a child worried about his grandparents' health and wanted to grow up quickly to help them. Another child wrote that he liked to sing, and talked about the desire to become a singer, but "my family doesn't have the money, so my dream may never come true."

"I wish I could help them more," Lin said.

Lin traveled to Harvard University and the Massachusetts Institute of Technology to attend advanced training courses for charitable leaders and met many foreign charitable people. He asked them if there were any institutions like Red Apple Public Welfare abroad, and they answered that they didn't know.

He checked the Internet only to find some similar small public welfare institutions in the United States, which mostly just provide psychological counseling. He presumed that the demands were different because of the different national conditions. He couldn't find many examples to refer to when it came to helping children of inmates. Sometimes he would feel like the old Chinese idiom "crossing the river by feeling the stones" in which each step he took was a step into the unknown, and he didn't know how to move forward.

Red Apple Public Welfare's funds are still stretched due to the need to help more than 2,000 children, with an annual subsidy of 1000-3000 yuan for each child, which is only a drop in the sea for these families.

But Lin is confident about the future. The group is getting more and more attention. He hopes the "red apple model" will be followed across China to benefit more children.

为流浪者流浪

Finding Homes for the Homeless

作者：胡　宁
翻译：吴爱俊

为流浪者流浪

蔡艳球红了，这是他生命中的意外事件。

蔡艳球出生于江西九江一个普通农民家庭，初中文化，长得不帅，不善言辞。这个“85后”没有任何才艺，“唱歌不是一般难听”。他发微博时经常写错别字，演讲稿都是粉丝帮忙写的。在直播的世界里，蔡艳球的名字叫“牛哥”，是一个彻头彻尾的“非主流”。在以蓝光画质著称的某直播平台上，他的直播间常年只能维持最低的清晰度，还时常对不上焦。

他直播的内容也和光鲜亮丽搭不上边，大多是灰头土脸的流浪者。蔡艳球与他们交流，希望送他们回家。他开辟的“寻找救助流浪者”直播间，在一众美颜、游戏、才艺直播中独树一帜。

蔡艳球第一次见大场面是在一次公开的演讲活动中。当时，他身边站着俞灏明、大鹏等明星，台下坐着上百位观众。他向现场的观众说起自己刚开始直播时的困惑：“直播我是看过，可直播救助流浪者能有人看吗？”

事实上，他的叫作“牛哥追梦”的直播间订阅人数已超过32万。起初还很冷清的直播间，如今只要开播，弹幕就不会停。挂着“追梦团”粉丝徽章的观众名单变得越来越长。靠直播时的礼物收入，蔡艳球已经能维持基本生活开支。他的粉丝微信群已经建到了第六个。

穿着粉丝为他制作的红色马甲，蔡艳球每天开着车奔走在城乡接合部。江西、福建、安徽、湖南、广东，桥洞下、烂尾楼里、乡道边上、公厕里……他走了两年，专程寻找这些明明存在却被多数人视若无睹的流浪者。自2016年底至2018年年初，蔡艳球已成功为38名流浪者找到了家。

为了方便称呼，每一个流浪者都会被直播间的粉丝赋予一个代号。刚被蔡艳球送回家的流浪者是开封人，于是被称为“开封哥”。还有一位流浪者总背着女士包，于是被称作“背包哥”。

第33位成功回家的流浪者被称为丁老师。他住在福建省建瓯市的一座桥下。堆成山的垃圾其实是他赖以维生的“行李”。他的皱纹里都是灰尘，紫色的棉袄蹭得乌黑锃亮。他下意识地跟陌生的蔡艳球保持距离。

蔡艳球像一个侦探。他通过与流浪者交谈，听口音分辨其家乡所在地。他拿笔让他们写下名字和家庭情况，观察他们生活里的蛛丝马迹，比如丁老师带在身边的两本书。比对字迹后他发现，丁老师可能来自浙江省台州市天台县赤山村。于是，蔡艳球与粉丝分头寻找当地的派出所、村委会等联系方式，搜索网上的寻人信息，大家共同鉴别真假，很快就联系上了丁老师的家人。丁老师的故事由此揭开：走失25年以上，曾做过教师，精神出问题后走失流浪，妻子已经改嫁……有些细节蔡艳球也不甚清楚，但是最重要的是，流浪者不再是断线的风筝。回归家庭，意味着他们重新融入社会有了一丝可能。

蔡艳球有车有房，也有远方牵挂他的妻

子和女儿，但是为了寻找这些流浪者，他很少能安定下来。有时他也会像流浪者一样头发油腻，手指甲里、脸上都是脏污。那辆二手车是床，也是移动仓库。他在车上准备了剪刀和锅：剪刀用来帮流浪者剪发，让他们看起来精神些；锅用来煮些清汤面。

车子常常“闹脾气”，把他扔在渺无人烟的荒郊。他每天吃住都在车上，只有需要带流浪者洗澡的时候，他才会去小宾馆开个20元一位的房间。12元一碗的盖浇饭，算是他吃得最奢侈的“大餐”了。

最难受的时候是夏天。蚊子嗡嗡地叫一整夜，并在他身上留下大大小小的包。夏天酷热，晒了一天的车子里更闷热难耐。为了节省油钱，他很少开空调。如果半夜太热，他就洗把脸。想洗头洗澡时，他就找个人少的野外用毛巾擦身。

他的生活极似苦行僧，但他还是没有停下来的打算。他的哥哥患有癫痫，“从小智力不如常人”。在哥哥17岁那年的正月里，一家人走亲戚拜年。下雨天，一行人打着伞走路，在弯弯绕绕的路上把她的哥哥弄丢了。哥哥迷路了。那时候还是少年的蔡艳球跟家人一起足足找了三天。但是找到哥哥时，哥哥已经“不行了”。

蔡艳球有时会想，如果当时有谁能帮帮走失的哥哥，也许哥哥现在还活得好好的呢。

在直播生涯开始之前，他因家中变故负债，常年在外跑小生意。有一阵子，他上午做生意，下午帮流浪者回家。结果，“生意没做好，流浪者也没帮到”。

直到一位做直播的朋友给出建议，他才知道还可以直播救助流浪汉。朋友告诉他，如果有人打赏礼物，他也能得到些补贴。什么都不会的蔡艳球开始得举步维艰，家中还有妻子和两个女儿要靠他养活，他的债务至今没有还清。

他因害羞从不主动向粉丝要礼物，但是每次收到礼物他都非常开心。那些礼物保障着他妻儿的衣食住行，也是他继续寻找流浪汉的物质基础。

除了直播间的礼物，蔡艳球很少接受其他馈赠。他的粉丝目睹了两年间蔡艳球数次拒绝流浪者亲属递上来的感谢红包。一次避让红包的过程中，蔡艳球不慎踩到一块钉板上刺伤了脚。粉丝想给他众筹换一辆质量好的车，但他拒绝接受，宁可自己借钱、贷款。

“老牛就是犟。”50岁的施正水在蔡艳球开播两个月时就成为了观众。让他印象深刻的是，这头“犟牛”不到办法用尽就是不放弃，有时候为了一个流浪者找个十天半月也在所不惜。

比起成功，寻找过程中的无奈更多。蔡艳球曾在广东帮助了两个20多岁的小伙子。第二天，当他预备开车送这俩小伙子去车站时，却发现前一天给他们买车票的钱被他们挥霍在了网吧。他去劝他们，3天后，小伙子依然安坐在网吧的卡座里，直到车票钱又被用完。其中一个小伙子腿受了伤，却宁愿坐在网吧打游戏也不愿拿钱回家治病。

让更多粉丝无法忘记的是“舞哥”。他住在一个烂尾楼里，每日跟周围居民散养的牲畜睡在一起，刺鼻的味道他浑然不觉。饿了，他就去旁边的垃圾箱里找吃的。在他的小房间里，整齐地摆放着拾来的棉被和衣物。不过，他却不懂得用，还是睡在光秃秃的木板上。

他冲着蔡艳球笑，但一言不发。蔡艳球一度以为他不会说话，直到3天后蔡艳球放音乐时才看到了一丝希望——流浪者随着音乐笨拙地舞动四肢，还跟着咿咿呀呀唱起了歌。“舞哥”之名由此而来。

蔡艳球能做的到此为止。他无法问出更多信息。就连走到街对面这短短几米，舞哥都极易受刺激。半个月后，蔡艳球不得不跟舞哥告别。这些没被成功送回家的流浪者，化作一条条笔记，以照片和定位的形式保存在他的手机记录里。

“我是一个普通人。”他再三强调。他没有能力帮助零星分布在城市边缘的每个流浪者。他只能扮演一个偌大的国度里“小小的补丁”，将情况反映给当地的救助站，再借官方的力量庇护这些无所归依的人。蔡艳球说：“我个人能力非常小，真正帮他们需要全社会的力量。”

这种想法也贯彻到蔡艳球选择“房管”（一般的直播间里，刷礼物到一定数额，主播会给该粉丝管理员权限，能够禁言、管理普通粉丝——作者注）的标准中。蔡艳球只看这位粉丝能否热心帮忙维护直播间、寻找流浪者出身的线索，来决定是否给他“房管”。31位“房管”如今也成为了“普通人牛哥”的三头六臂，他们是帮他化解孤独寂寞的旅伴，甚至是比他更有能力的寻找者。

通过直播信号扯起的巨大网络，正在兜住越来越多的流浪者。蔡艳球的粉丝有着与一般直播间截然不同的年龄结构：多数在30岁以上，工薪阶层，很少有“土豪”。

在成为蔡艳球的粉丝之前，他们都不大关注生活中出现的流浪者。但如今，有的粉丝主动向他提供线索，还有的按照蔡艳球的方式成功帮助流浪者回家。当蔡艳球遇到流浪者说他听不懂的方言时，天南海北的粉丝就是他的翻译。一旦出现流浪者家乡的线索，粉丝们就像是蔡艳球的“移动秘书”，一起寻找可能的信息、线索，并一一求证。

蔡艳球平等地看待这些流浪者，有时甚至“忘记他们身上有味道”。粉丝们也被他感染，主动给发现的流浪者送吃送喝，而不是掩鼻快速经过。

“牛哥（蔡艳球）让我看到，流浪者就是中国最底层的人。我们看了这两年的直播以后，觉得他们是很善良、有尊严的人，不会向你乞讨。他们就是找不到回家的路而已。”粉丝邹鲁描述着他对流浪者的看法。

这是农民、小生意人蔡艳球此前从没体会到的成就感。“我从一个普通人变成了一个小公众人物吧。”

蔡艳球说自己为流浪汉“流浪”了七万公里，但依然前路未知。他不确定旅程将持续多久。“我想有更多时间陪家人和小孩。可能以后流浪者很少的时候，我就回家了。”蔡艳球还面临着身份上的尴尬：既不是公职人员，也不是志愿者，在查找、联系家人时会有一些麻烦。生活上的困难依然存在。两个孩子都要上学，家中的开销可能水涨船高。不过直播间的粉丝们总希望他能一直坚持下去。

至少，现在蔡艳球仍在寻找、救助之路上兴致勃勃。他记得，有一位流浪者在外20多年，当流浪者的弟弟连夜赶到时，蔡艳球才知道，这位流浪者的老父母“已经在街上寻找了他20多年”。当时，蔡艳球跟家属都激动得流泪了。他想着，如果能重回哥哥走失那年，他希望哥哥也能遇到一个“蔡艳球”，给他吃的，送他回家。

Finding Homes for the Homeless

Cai Yanqiu has become popular, which is something he never expected.

He was born in the late eighties into an ordinary farming family in Jiujiang, Jiangxi Province. He graduated from junior middle school. He is not handsome or eloquent, doesn't have any talent and "sings badly." In his social media posts, you can often see typos. When he gives speeches, they are written by fans. In his live streaming platform, Cai calls himself "Brother Niu." On a live streaming platform known for its high quality, his broadcast is at the lowest resolution, and is often out of focus.

The content of his live broadcast is not about glamor or beauty, but about the homeless. He tries to help these people, and communicates with them with the hope of encouraging them to return home. "Finding and Returning the Homeless" is an entirely different sort of program content from "normal" ones about cosmetics, games and talent shows.

It was the first time for him to meet so many people at a public speech. Stars like Yu Haoming (Ham) and Da Peng (Dong Chengpeng) stood beside him across from several hundred people in the audience. He talked about why he started his program. "I've seen many live programs, but never anything about how to help the homeless."

His live broadcast channel is called "Brother Niu Chases Dreams," and has over 320,000 subscribers. In the beginning, no one watched. But now, everyone watches and the comments never stop, and more and more fans are joining every day. During broadcasts, fans give money, and Cai can rely on this revenue to maintain basic living expenses. He has six WeChat groups of fans.

Cai wears the red waistcoat made by his fans and drives through the countryside and cities every day. From the end of 2016 to the beginning of 2018, he traveled across Jiangxi, Fujian, Anhui, Hunan, and Guangdong provinces. He has found homes for 38 homeless people living under bridges, on the roadside, in dilapidated houses and public bathrooms.

When the program starts, each homeless person is quickly given a nickname by the fans. One man was from Kaifeng, so he was called "Brother Kaifeng." Another always wore a lady's bag, so he was called "Brother Bag."

The 33rd homeless person helped by Cai was called Teacher Ding, and he'd lived under a bridge in Jian'ou, Fujian Province. He lived with piles of rubbish. There was dust in his wrinkles. His purple coat was becoming dirty black. While in Cai's program, it was clear he was uneasy, and subconsciously kept himself away at a distance.

When talking to them on his show, Cai is like a detective. He can deduce where someone comes from by identifying his accent. He will also ask them to write down their names and family background, and will slowly find out other clues about their lives. For example, Teacher Ding brought two books with him to the show. From these books and the words Teacher Ding wrote, Cai deduced that he had come from the village of Chishan near Taizhou in Zhejiang Province. Cai and his fans then contacted the local police station and village committee and searched for information about Teacher Ding online. Soon, they found some members of his family. It turned out that Ding used to be a teacher, and had been missing for over 25 years. He'd suffered from mental illness, went missing, and his wife got re-married. Cai is not entirely clear about all the details of his background. What is important, however, is that he has returned home, which means there is still a chance for him to reintegrate into society.

Cai constantly travels, and is away from his wife and daughters most of the time. They miss him very much. But he does this work to help these homeless people. Sometimes, it's almost like he himself is homeless, with his oily hair and dust beneath his nails and on his face. His second-hand car is his bed as well as a mobile warehouse. He keeps scissors and a pot in the car to give haircuts to the homeless and to cook noodles for them.

His car often breaks down in deserted, remote areas. He eats and sleeps in his car. Only when he meets a homeless person who needs a bath does he pay 20 yuan for a bed in a small hotel, and 12 yuan for a bowl of rice with meat and vegetables. This is considered an extravagant "feast."

Summer is the worst time. Mosquitoes buzz and bite him all night, leaving large welts on his skin. Summer is also scorching hot, so staying in the car is unbearable. To save gas money, he rarely uses the air-conditioner. If it's too hot during the midnight, he'll wash his face to cool down. If he wants to bathe, he'll find a sparsely populated area to wash his body with a towel.

He is as poor as a monk, but he has no plans to stop. He once had an elder brother, who has since passed away. It was during a New Year's holiday when Cai and his family went to visit relatives. That day happened to be a rainy day. As all of them were walking along a winding path with umbrellas, his brother, just 17 years old, suddenly went missing. His brother had epilepsy, and was also slightly mentally handicapped. Cai and his family spent three days looking for him. When they finally found him, he was already near death. He died shortly afterwards.

Cai often thinks that if someone had helped his missing brother, he might still be alive today.

Before he began his live broadcast, he would do some small jobs to pay off his family debt. Over time, he would do jobs in the morning and then help homeless people in the afternoon. But doing the jobs did not help very much, and he also couldn't help the homeless people much, either.

He had no idea that a live program could help homeless people until one of his friends suggested it to him. His friend said that fans often give money. In the beginning, the program did not go very smoothly. This was worrying to him, as he had a wife and two daughters depending on him to support them, and he also had outstanding debts to pay.

He's too shy to ask his fans for virtual gifts, so he's very happy when they send them. The gifts help him pay for transportation, food, clothing and shelter for his wife and children, and provide the material support for him to continue helping the homeless.

Except for the money Cai receives from his live program, he seldom accepts other donations. His fans have seen how he routinely refuses the "red envelopes" (traditional gifts of money) offered as gratitude by relatives of homeless people whom Cai has helped. Once, when refusing a red envelope, he even accidentally stepped on a nail in a board and seriously hurt his foot. Another time, fans offered to crowdsource in order to buy him a new car, but he refused their offer, preferring to buy a car by getting a loan instead.

"Brother Niu is stubborn," said 50-year-old Shi Zhengshui, who became a fan after the program was about two months old. What strikes him most is that Cai never gives up, and will "even spend ten or fifteen days looking for the information of a homeless person."

There are more failures than successes in Cai's mission to help the homeless. He once found two young men around 20 years old in Guangdong. He gave them money to buy train tickets to return home, but the next day when he was about to take them to the train station, he discovered they'd spent all the money at an internet café. He gave them money again, and urged them not to squander it, but three days later the two men had again spent all the train ticket money at the internet café. One of them had an injured leg, but he preferred to play games at the internet café rather than return home to treat his leg.

Another homeless man that his fans will never forget was "Dance Brother." He lived in a dilapidated house where local people raised livestock. He was used to the foul odor of the livestock. When hungry, he would go to a nearby trash bin for food. In his small room, the cotton quilts and clothing he picked up were neatly folded. However, he still slept on a bare wooden board because he didn't know what the quilts were for.

When Cai found him, the man had smiled at Cai but remained speechless, making Cai think he couldn't speak. Three days later, however, Cai saw a glimmer of hope when he was playing some music and the man began waving his arms and legs and even sang along. He was thus nicknamed "Dance Brother."

Though he tried, Cai could not discover any information about Dance Brother, who would become easily irritated just walking down the street together. Two weeks passed like this, until Cai finally had to say goodbye. For those he can't help, Cai still has pictures of them on his phone.

"I am an ordinary person," Cai said again and again. He can't help every homeless person he finds. In such a big country, he is just one person. All he can do is to report homeless people to local rescue centers, and provide shelter if he can. "My capacity is limited," he said. "We need everyone in society to help."

When choosing "online managers" [1] from fans, Cai considers if a fan can maintain order of his live show or if he is good at finding out information about the homeless person in question. Cai currently has 36 online managers. They help him relieve his loneliness and are even better at finding homeless people than he is.

---

1 Generally speaking, if fans give a certain amount of money to the host, the host will grant them "manager status" to manage fans or even ban comments during a live program.

Cai has been able to expand his helping the homeless using the internet. Unlike fans on other live programs, most of his fans are working class people over 30 years old, not the nouveau rich or "tycoons."

Before watching Cai's program, his fans didn't pay any attention to homeless people. But now, some fans will even provide Cai with information about some homeless people, and some even help them find their homes. When Cai encounters a homeless person who speaks a dialect he can't understand, fans will help translate. Whenever clues appear about the hometown of a homeless person, fans are like Cai's "mobile secretaries," communicating with one another to find more clues and verify them together.

Cai looks at these homeless people as equals, and sometimes is even oblivious to their foul smell. Because of this, his fans have also changed their own behavior to the homeless, sometimes offering them food rather than passing by quickly while holding their noses.

"Brother Niu shows us that the homeless are the bottom of society in China. Having watched the live broadcast for two years, I feel that these people are kind and dignified because they never beg from you. They just cannot find their way home," one of his fans, Zou Lu, observed.

Cai Yanqiu, a farmer and small businessman, has never felt such a sense of achievement. "I have turned from a common person into a public figure."

Cai said he had traveled some 70,000 kilometers helping homeless people, but he was still unsure when his journey would end. “I want to spend more time with my family and children. Perhaps when there are just a few homeless, I can return home.” Since he is neither a public servant nor a volunteer, it is not easy for him to contact the families of these homeless people. He also faces an enormous life burden. He has to afford school tuition for his two children and an ever-increasing living costs. However, fans all hope that he can stick to his mission.

For now, Cai is indeed sticking with it. He still remembers one particular homeless man he helped. When Cai brought him home, and the man’s younger brother rushed out to meet him, that was when Cai was told that the man’s parents had been looking for him for over 20 years. At that moment, Cai and the family were moved to tears. Cai wished, when his own brother had been lost, he could have met a similar “Cai Yanqiu,” who would have also given him food and helped him find his way home.

刻在生命里的生命热线

The Life Hotline Worth Living For

作者：江　山
翻译：卢　敏

刻在生命里的生命热线

曹文英的世界正在一点一点缩小。小儿麻痹症的后遗症把她锁在成都家里不到3平方米的床上，56年的卧床时间让她的心肺功能越来越差，咀嚼和吞咽对她来说也非易事。她全身瘫痪，依靠60岁的丈夫才能活动，丈夫出去工作时她不敢喝水吃饭，因为90岁的父母已无力再移动她。

她的体重在不断减轻。她剩余的几乎全部力量都被她用在那部电话上。

电话是1999年开通的。那时曹文英和同样因为小儿麻痹症瘫痪的妹妹开通了“曹氏生命热线”，专门为陷入困境的人提供咨询和帮助。

不断响起的来电仿佛在书写着一部人生问题的百科全书。从青年的恋爱烦恼到中年夫妻离异、出轨、家暴问题，为这些事犯难的人纷纷打电话给她们。有耄耋老人打电话诉说孩子不赡养自己，还有7岁的孩子怯生生地问她，想为开出租车的父母分担点家务，打扫卫生时不小心打碎一只花瓶怎么办……

一天深夜，她们接到一位男士的电话，他倾诉的是无法接受自己是同性恋的苦恼。曹文英傻了眼，那时刚刚进入21世纪，在中国，同性恋话题依然隐匿而神秘，她根本不知道该如何应对。她打电话给认识的大学生，询问他们对同性恋的看法。最后她得出结论："同性恋不是病，只是一种状态。"当男子再次打来电话时，她如此告诉对方，结果，从电话中传来了哭声。

2005年，与她相依为命多年的妹妹因为肺衰、心衰离开人世，她也在同年被医生下了死亡通知单，预测寿命只剩下两年。

她一度想关停"生命热线"。电话打进来时，她总是会想起妹妹，心里堵得慌，但她却只能强忍着悲痛去宽慰别人。她在报纸上登出自己这一想法，一位16岁的打工小伙儿打电话过来，带着恳求的口气说"能不能不要关，我给你打钱"。曹文英最后还是放弃了这一念头，只是，以前的"曹氏生命热线”变成了孤零零的“曹文英生命热线”。

后来，“曹文英生命热线”的名气逐渐大了，海报也进了校园、上了报纸、上了网站。只要打进电话，她来者不拒。而在电话线的那头，许多人并不知道，给予他们希望的声音来自一位全身瘫痪的残疾人。

曹文英4个月大的时候就因为罹患小儿麻痹症而瘫痪。但在生命的头20多年里，她始终憋着一口气学习、治病。她最喜欢教师、医生这两个职业。

那时，当地流行一种“穴位强刺激疗法”，即在肩胛、股肱主要的穴位打上麻药，用刀子割开，直接刺激主干神经，“像和饺子馅一样搅”。麻药失效，曹文英痛得死去活来。她不喊，心里想着，治好病就能和同龄的孩子一样上学去。剧痛之下肢体出现的应激反应一度让家人惊喜，但是最终收效甚微。

辗转几家医院后，和曹文英同一个院子长大的伙伴都上了学，喜好文学的曹文英的胳膊依然举不起来，妹妹的双腿也无法动弹。

没法去上学，姐妹俩就查字典认字，读哥哥的课本自学，在家里合写文章投稿。后来，她们的作品发表在当地报纸上，许多人写信来交流。一个残疾小伙子讲述自己的女朋友家庭无法接受他，信的末尾写着：“3天内收不到你们的回信，我就要离开这个世界。”在拆阅信件时，信已经寄来一星期了，曹文英和妹妹赶忙回复，然而过了不久，这个小伙子的家人回信说他已经自杀了。

这件事极大地触动了曹文英姐妹俩，“如果有部电话机就好了”。提出这个想法后，父母觉得“只要她们能开心”就好，于是掏了3600元，接来一根电话线，从此曹文英开始了在电话机旁长达19年的坚守。

出乎意料的是，打电话来咨询的人不少。一部白色的老式电话机在她们的枕头旁边摆着，铃声一响，妹妹曹文君马上拿起电话接听。曹文英和曹文君一个白天接，一个夜晚接。“这个热线就好像是一扇我们了解世界、了解社会的窗口，让我们明白这个世界上还有许多不幸的人，还有比我们更不幸的人。”

给她们打电话的人各种各样。有工地上干活的年轻小伙儿，也有大学里的教师。从没进过一天校园的曹文英担心自己没水平辅导别人。她买来心理学教材苦读，但是一接电话还是发现，“要是照着心理学教程就做不了这个”。

2002年，一位男子打电话过来，说自己明天想要自杀。她一下子蒙了，又马上镇定下来，告诉对方“你如果真的要死，明天也要打电话告诉我妹妹一声”，她希望用这个方式拖住他。第二天这通电话没有如约而至。姐妹俩很着急，根据对方透露的一些线索，一个单位一个单位打电话去问，可对方用的是化名，音信全无。

直到一天晚上，这个男人才再次打电话过来，道歉说那天过后他就没再想这件事，直到听说姐妹俩在找他。

为寻找这个人，曹文英家的电话费花了100多元。有人劝她们不必花这冤枉钱，她一开始也有些气恼，但转念一想，如果100多元能换一条生命，那这钱就花得值！

她逐渐摸索出自己的一套方法，关键的

秘诀是“看人、看事真要用心”。一些人打来电话就骂骂咧咧、语无伦次，她会好言好语地安抚对方，让他一点一点讲，末了自己再总结，问一句“你想表达的是不是这个意思”。

只要有电话打来，几小时她都陪着聊。她曾经创下的纪录是聊了58个小时，对方喋喋不休地说着他朋友的爱情悲剧，曹文英在电话线这边陪着一起长吁短叹，只有对方吃饭或者上卫生间时，她才能抽出空隙来解决自己的问题。

妹妹去世后，曹文英没法自己拿听筒，就新配了一部手机。要用手机时，她只能像一只布偶一样被家人摆弄着，右手卡着手机，靠在两个枕头上，头往右倾斜，左手一直举到额头上，向外翻转弯曲，将触屏笔夹在虎口、顶着屏幕，才能用有限的力气点触。要把笔挪到其他位置，曹文英得调动左脸的肌肉，夸张地努着嘴，才能让触屏笔前进几毫米。

即便如此，每当她发现打电话来的人需要更多帮助时，她都会主动让他们加她的微信语音或视频聊天，并解释说“这样就不会浪费你的电话费了”。

“生命热线”开通以来，她从没收过一分钱。有人冷嘲热讽地说，“只有傻子才不要钱”。在她看来，“正是因为我不收费，才会有那么多的电话。实际上真正需要帮的恰恰就是这些人”。

19年来，咨询者换了一拨儿又一拨儿，在他们身上，曹文英感觉自己见证了社会的变化。他们问的问题越来越多，要求也越来越高。以往曹文英坚持“不给他们做主，只是给一个建议”，但是现在在电话里，急躁的成年人会大声嚷嚷着“你就告诉我，我到底该怎么做”，渴望得到一个现成的答案。

更多的时候她接受的是情感问题咨询。原先曹文英觉得学历高的人很聪明，一点就透，现在发现他们根本不动脑筋，没有一点耐心。她觉得奇怪：“他们太缺乏沟通意识，跟别人说话滔滔不绝的，可是为什么对着最亲近的人没话说？”

有的人解决了问题就销声匿迹，再无音讯。有的人成了她的朋友，时不时来看望她。

新的电话依然源源不断。

曹文英也能够理解这些人的心情，“作为残疾人，社会对我没有那么高的要求，但是他们作为健全人，上有老下有小，要面对的是整个世界”。

“生命热线”出名后，曹文英被人叫作“四川张海迪”，她不愿意。1983年，张海迪的事迹在全中国传播。当时，20岁出头的曹文英留着长发，被人挖苦：“其他不像张海迪，外表倒是挺像。”张海迪给她带来动力，更是巨大的压力。

那时她性格内向、拧巴，不愿说话，心里常常气得不行。“张海迪瘫痪后下身一点知觉都没有，我虽然不能动，但神经都是好的。”用她的话来说，“一根头发丝拂过皮肤”都能感觉到。夏天是最难熬的，蚊子在她腿上猛劲儿吸着血，她只能盯着看，或喊母亲过来帮她赶跑。

如今，曹文英把“生命热线”当成了自己的事业，她更有底气说，“我就是曹文英”，因为“张海迪做到的事我没有做到，我做到的事张海迪也没做，你不能把两件事扯到一起”。

“我是没办法，如果我手脚健全，一定有更多的工作可以做。”

没进校园念书成了她始终耿耿于怀的事。但她觉得“有了这个热线，我们知道了我们的价值所在，知道了我们具备的能力，还知道我们不是废人，不是没有用的人，不是社会的包袱，也不是父母的累赘”。

曹文英还通过电话结识了现在的丈夫姚双全。姚双全童年家庭不幸，出门打工又遭欺负。他在收音机中听说了曹文英的“生命热线”后打电话来咨询。当时曹文英追求者众多，但是她看中姚双全支持她继续自己“生命热线”的事业，于是决定嫁给他。

依靠60岁的丈夫抱着背着，曹文英才能挪出那张小床。但这一过程也显得惊心动魄。尽管她的体重现在只有七八十斤重，但丈夫姚双全告诉记者，“不像抱一件70斤重的东西”，如果重心控制不得当，曹文英就有可能一下子栽到地上。

丈夫去上班的时间里，她即使接电话讲到嘴角泛起白沫也不肯喝一口水，“怕解手”。现在，她内心的全部担忧是，丈夫今年就要退休，家中的全部开支只靠老父亲的退休工资难以为继，但若丈夫再找一份全日制工作，她的处境将会更加困难。

她还是无法放弃“生命热线”。她发誓，“只要我的生命存在一天，我的‘生命热线’就会存在一天”。

一位曾经得到过她帮助的中年男子说起“曹老师”满是钦佩。他去看过曹文英，佩服她比许多健康的人更“看得开”。在曹文英看来，“我帮他们不觉得亏了，我在他们身上学到了许多我在书本上学不到的东西。我失去的东西远远不如我得到的多”。

她承认，19年前，她并没有今天这么豁达。年轻的时候，她不是没想到过死，但是她绝望地发现自己“连自杀的能力都没有”。开通“生命热线”后，这个念头渐渐消失了，她发现自己琢磨更多的是怎么把别人从死亡边缘拉回来。

她说自己还有很多梦想没有实现。她想去看海，想带90岁的父母亲回趟老家。命运却从未给她和家人一天喘息的机会。

她始终记得自己第一次出远门的情形。

那是1991年，河北唐山老家亲戚来信，邀请他们回故乡看看。曹文英和妹妹坐着火车，颠簸了两天两夜，一路往北回到家乡。小侄女推着她们的轮椅在田埂上跑得飞快，采下路边的野花撒在她们身上。她们把花儿带回家，仔仔细细地插在窗台上的花瓶里。

一天黄昏时分，她看到远处地平线上一轮巨大的红日滚滚坠地，夕照泼洒在绿浪一样的田野上，天地寂静，田野广阔，青烟袅袅上升。她第一次感觉到，在自然面前，自己的痛苦不值一提。

那一刻，她和命运和解了。她暗暗地想："人早晚要死，但是应该顺其自然，不要自己去结束。每个人来到世界上都有自己的价值，如果我们一天天消沉下去，就是白来到世界上一趟。"

The Life Hotline Worth Living For

Cao Wenying's world is shrinking little by little. She is 56 years old, and still suffers from the after effects of polio, and is confined to her small bed in her home in Chengdu. A lifetime of lying in bed has worsened the functions of her heart and lungs. Chewing and swallowing are difficult. She is paralyzed and relies on her 60-year-old husband to move her around. When he goes to work, she does not dare eat or drink because her 90-year-old parents cannot move her.

She is losing weight. She uses almost all of her remaining strength to talk on the phone.

Her phone service, called "Cao's Life Hotline," was begun in 1999. It provides specialist advice and help for those in trouble. It was started by Cao and her younger sister Cao Wenjun, who was also paralyzed due to polio.

The constant calls constitute an encyclopedia of life issues. From the love troubles of young people to the issues of middle-aged couples like divorce, infidelity and domestic violence, people would call Cao and her sister for advice. Some senior citizens would call to complain that their children weren't taking care of them. A seven-year-old child called them once. She wanted to share some housework with her parents, who are taxi drivers, but accidentally broke a vase while cleaning the house. She asked what she should do.

One night, they received a phone call from a distressed man who confided that he was not able to accept he was gay. Cao Wenying was perplexed. At the turn of the 21st century, the topic of homosexuality was still unspoken in China, and she didn't know how to deal with it. She called university students she knew and asked what they thought of homosexuality. In the end, she concluded that homosexuality was not a disease, but rather biological in nature. When the man called again, she told him. Hearing that, he began to cry on the phone.

In 2005, her younger sister passed away due to lung and heart failure. In the same year, the doctor also told Cao that she would live for only two more years.

For a time, she considered shutting down the "Life Hotline." Whenever there was a phone call, she would think of her younger sister. But she endured her grief in order to comfort others. Her story appeared in the newspaper, and a 16-year-old migrant worker called her and pleaded, "Can you continue to operate the life hotline? I'll give you money." Cao Wenying gave up the idea of quitting, but the former "Cao's Life Hotline" became "Cao Wenying's Life Hotline".

Gradually, her hotline became well-known, and posters for it could be seen on campuses, in newspapers, and on websites. She will not refuse any call. On the other end of the phone line, many people don't know that the voice that gives them hope comes from a paralyzed person.

When four-month-old Cao Wenying suffered from polio, she became paralyzed. For the first 20 years of her life, she tried her best to study and cure her condition. Because of this, she likes the two professions of teacher and doctor most.

At that time, “strong acupoint stimulation therapy” was popular in her city. It involved injecting anesthetics into the main acupoints of the shoulder blade, arm and thigh, cutting them with a knife, and directly stimulating the central nerve. The anesthetic was ineffective, and Cao was in great pain, but she didn't scream. She thought if she were cured, she could go to school like other children her age. In the end, however, the therapy had little effect.

While she was undergoing medical treatment in several hospitals, the other children who grew up with her in the same courtyard continued going to school. Cao, however, couldn't even raise her arms, and her younger sister couldn't move her legs.

But Cao loved literature. Because they couldn't go to school, the two sisters would look up Chinese characters in the dictionary to be literate. They would also read their elder brother's textbooks to study on their own, and wrote articles together at home to contribute to newspapers. Later, their articles were published in local newspapers, and many people wrote letters to them. A disabled young man told them his girlfriend's family would not accept him. At the end of the letter, he wrote, “If I don't receive your reply within three days, I will leave this world.” When they read the letter, they realized it'd been sent a week ago. Cao and her younger sister quickly replied, but the young man's family later replied that he had already committed suicide.

This shocked the two sisters. “It'd be better if we had a phone.” After they mentioned the idea, their parents felt it would be fine “as long as they're happy.” They paid 3,600 yuan and obtained a phone line. Cao then used the phone line for 19 years.

Soon and unexpectedly, people began calling for advice. An old-fashioned white phone was placed next to their pillows. As soon as it rang, her younger sister would immediately answer it. They decided to take phone calls in shifts. "This life hotline is like a window for us to know more about the world and society, and see that there are many unfortunate people in the world, some of whom are more unfortunate than us."

People from different walks of life called them, such as young people working on construction sites and university teachers. Since Cao was not a student of psychology, she was worried that she could not give good advice to others. She bought psychology textbooks to study, but when she answered the phone, she felt that she was competent enough.

In 2002, a man called and said that he wanted to commit suicide the next day. Cao was stunned but immediately calmed down, telling him, "If you really want to die, you should call my younger sister tomorrow." She hoped to delay his suicide this way. The next day, he did not make the call. The two sisters were very anxious. According to some clues disclosed by the man, they called each possible workplace, but the man used a pseudonym, and there was no information about him.

One night, the man called again. He told them that he hadn't thought about committing suicide ever since, and he was sorry that the two sisters had been looking for him.

Cao spent more than 100 yuan on phone bills trying to find him. Some people advised them not to spend the money. She was a little annoyed at first, but she thought that if 100 yuan can save a life, then it was worth it.

She gradually figured out her own methods, and the key was to consider each person with great care. When some called, they would curse and speak incoherently. She would persuade them to calm down and talk in detail. In the end, she would sum up what they said and ask, "Is this what you wanted to express?"

As long as there was a phone call, she would chat for hours. She once set a record of talking for 58 hours. The caller was chattering about his friend's love tragedy. Cao Wenying sighed with him on the phone line. Only when the caller ate or went to the toilet could she take a break to handle her own things.

After her younger sister died, Cao didn't have the strength to hold the receiver herself, so she bought a mobile phone. When talking, her family had to help position her body. The mobile phone was stuck in her right hand, and she leaned on two pillows, with her head tilted to the right, and her left hand raised to her forehead and bent outwards. The touchscreen was in her hand between her thumb and index finger, and the screen touch pen was in her mouth. She was able to touch the screen with limited strength. To move the screen pen to another position, she had to mobilize the muscles of her left cheek and pout her lips to move the pen several millimeters.

Whenever she found that callers needed more help, she would add their WeChat. "In this way, you won't spend too much money on your phone bill."

Since the "Life Hotline" was put into use, she has never charged a fee. Some people have criticized her saying, "Only fools don't charge any money," but she responded, "It is precisely because I don't charge a fee that I have so many calls. It is because these people really need my help."

Over the past 19 years, the questions and problems have been changing. Cao feels that she has been witnessing the changes in society. People ask more questions and have higher expectations of her. She used to insist on "making no decisions for them, but giving suggestions," but now impatient adults are prone to yell, "Just tell me what I should do!" and eager to get solutions from her.

She provides more consulting on emotional issues. At first, she thought that people who've received a higher education must be very clever and will quickly get the hint, but she found that they didn't use their minds and were impatient. She was puzzled and thought, "They talk to others endlessly. Why don't they talk to their family?"

Some people disappear after their problems are solved. Others become her friends and come to visit her from time to time. There are still endless new calls.

Cao understands these people. "Since I'm a disabled person, society does not set such high demands on me. But for other people, they have parents and children, and they have to face the world."

After her "Life Hotline" became well-known, Cao was called "Sichuan's Zhang Haidi," but she is unwilling to accept this. In 1983, Zhang Haidi's story as a paraplegic girl who became a writer spread throughout China. At that time, 20-year-old Cao had long hair and was ridiculed by other people who said, "She only looks like Zhang Haidi, but is nothing like her." Zhang Haidi brought her both motivation and pressure.

At that time, Cao was introverted, stubborn, unwilling to speak, and very angry at what they said. "Zhang Haidi is paralyzed from the chest down," she'd said. "Although I can't move, my nerves are in good condition." She said that she could feel "a strand of hair brushing across her skin." She found it hard to bear the summer season. Mosquitoes sucked blood on her legs. She could only stare at them and call her mother to come help her drive them away.

Now, Cao regards the "Life Hotline" as her career. She said with great confidence, "I am Cao Wenying. I didn't do what Zhang Haidi did, and Zhang Haidi didn't do what I have done. You can't compare the two."

"I have no alternative. If my hands and feet are in good condition, I must have more work to do."

She has always felt bad that she was never able to go to school to study. But she feels that "with this hotline, we know our value, the ability we have, and we also know that we are disabled, but not useless, and not a burden to society and our parents."

Cao met with her husband Yao Shuangquan through the phone. His family was very poor growing up, and he became a migrant worker and was often bullied. He heard about Cao Wenying's "Life Hotline" on the radio and called for advice. At that time, Cao had many suitors, but she loved Yao Shuangquan because he supported her in continuing her "Life Hotline" career, so she decided to marry him.

Relying on her 60-year-old husband to carry her in his arms or on his back, Cao could finally move out of her small bed. The process is unnerving. She only weighs 35 or 40kg now. Her husband said that it was unlike carrying a "35kg thing." If the center of gravity is not appropriately controlled, she could suddenly fall to the ground.

When her husband goes to work, she won't drink a sip of water because she is "afraid of going to the toilet." Now she is worried that her husband will retire this year, and all her family cannot live on the retirement salary of her elderly father. But if her husband finds another full-time job, her situation will be even more difficult.

She still can't give up the "Life Hotline." She vowed, "As long as I'm alive, my 'Life Hotline' will exist."

A middle-aged man she once helped talked about "Teacher Cao" with admiration. He had visited her in person, and admired her for being more "open-minded" than many healthy people. In Cao's view, "I feel I lose nothing by helping them. I learn a lot from them that I cannot study in books. My gains are more than my losses."

She admitted that 19 years ago, she was not as open-minded as she is today. When she was young, she thought about death, but she found that she could not commit suicide. After the "Life Hotline" was put into use, the idea gradually disappeared. She found herself thinking more about how to pull others back from the brink of death.

She says that she still had many unfulfilled dreams. She wants to see the sea, and she wants to take her 90-year-old parents back to her hometown. But fate never gives her and her family a chance to have a brief respite.

She always remembers the first time she went on a journey. In 1991, relatives from her hometown of Tangshan, Hebei Province wrote her a letter and invited Cao and her sister to visit. They took the train, traveling for two days and two nights, all the way north back to their hometown. Their little niece pushed them in their wheelchairs fast through the fields, plucking wildflowers from the roadside and sprinkling them on their bodies. They took the flowers home and carefully put them in vases on the windowsill.

At dusk, she saw the huge red sun on the horizon rolling down to the ground, and the evening glow was splashing on the green fields that ripples. The world was tranquil, the fields were vast, and the smoke curled up. For the first time in her life, she felt that in nature, all her pain had become insignificant.

At that moment, she reconciled with fate. "We will all die sooner or later, but we should let nature take its course instead of ending our lives by ourselves. Everyone has their own value in the world. If we sink down day by day, then we are living in this world for nothing."

富阳民间 110

Fuyang Civilian 110 Hotline

作者：杨　杰
翻译：卢　敏

富阳民间 110

他们被称作“民间 110”，他们不属于任何一支正规队伍。

他们的新“办公室”是公墓山前建起的两间房屋。杭州富阳野狼公益搜救队的“狼头”陈青伟做墓碑买卖，家里的门面房是搜救队的早期据点，一边摆着救援用的绳索，一边是样品骨灰盒。

队员几乎全来自农村。瓦匠、电焊工、猎人、酿酒的、养鸡的、卖二手车的、安装空调的、开小超市的、开烧烤店的、派出所协警、村卫生院医生，七七八八的人把自己装进统一的墨绿色队服，自掏腰包寻找失踪于山水间的人。

野狼搜救队的教练之一是孙海良，他是大型民间救援队——公羊队的正式成员，去过地震后的尼泊尔、台风后的莫桑比克。公羊队在全球有千名队员，救援设备包括声呐、潜水装备和一架直升机。

野狼队则几乎没有走出过富阳，救援集中在山地连绵的新登镇，装备包括一艘补丁缠身不得不“退役”的救生艇、自制的水下捞人铁钩，以及实施禁猎后从猎狗项圈上取下的定位装置。最具科技感的是一架无人机，还在一次夜晚搜救23名驴友的行动中丢失，葬身绿色丘陵地带。

跟天斗，跟地斗，最好还是退三步

教练孙海良不是爱冒险的人，只要有两成危险，他就不去挑战。每次穿上救援服，识别危险的雷达立马开启，“得先有危机感才能再去救人”。

他给“野狼”上的第一课就是如何保护自己。“千万不要跟自然抗争，跟天斗，跟地斗，最好还是退三步。”他的三个朋友是游泳高手，一次他们看到金沙江虎跳峡水流平稳就跳了下去，“差点儿没上来”，其中一个人眼看就要被水吞没，用尽最后一丝力气抱住了一块石头才幸免于难，从此他听到“金沙江”三个字便会不自觉地发抖。

“驴友的失踪也往往是因为盲目，没有真正去考量自己的体能，完成不可能的任务是对生命的挑战。”孙海良年轻的时候想当个小老板，或在国企里做领导。他现在每天坚持打太极，每个周末都外出散心。他还懂中医，拥有一家药店。

2008年，孙海良开始接触公益救援，3年前成为“野狼”的教练。他教队员们看等高线时不用专业术语，“纹路密集的地方就是悬崖，像树上的疤”。他还教他们如何急救、怎样用绳子岩降，但最重要的一课留给安全。他要求大家救落水者时一定不能毫无准备就单独下水，对方会把你当作最后一根稻草死命往下拽。“大家来做这个事情也不是为了赚钱，要是伤残了，你们的家人会不会伤心？”

孙海良每一次随公羊队出征都要签生死状，一切后果自己负责，跟国家和队伍无关。他参与了几次国际救援，常遇到别国的“熟面孔”，他们一个个都对危险保持警惕。“德国人很严谨，工具的大小和箱子都是严丝合缝的。”有一次五国救援队员联合演习，孙海良习惯性地把仪器靠墙，但日本人提出，在真实的野外，仪器要向外放，方便随时拖走。

云南鲁甸地震时，孙海良在田野的帐篷里给灾民量血压，余震来了，灾民拖着血压计就逃。灾区生活苦中作乐，灾民会拉着救援人员去家里吃饭，哪怕是在塌了一半的房间里喝一杯茶，主人都很高兴。救援结束时，当地的傣族人背来的花生、糯米把救援车前前后后塞得满满的。汽车发动，老人、小孩在路边跳起傣族舞，车子开了很远，他们还在跳。去西藏救灾时，孙海良的脖子上堆满了哈达。在尼泊尔救援结束临行前，人们朝他们摇头，大家开始时不解，后来才知道，在当地摇头表示尊敬。

孙海良今年 54 岁，膝盖因登山太多而凸起。前不久，他才参加完鄱阳湖水灾的救援，感慨体力不可避免地下降。“我最怕有一天，我报名参加救援，结果第一梯队没有我，第二梯队没有我，第三梯队还没有我。”

他始终记得自己第一次参与救援，失踪者是位 27 岁的小伙子，他是由妈妈独自他带大的。救援队员去山里搜寻，那位妈妈拿着快餐面等在一旁，见有人回来总是先问“儿子找到了吗”，大家摇头。她把快餐面端到大伙面前，说“你们辛苦了”。从第一天到第十一天，那位妈妈一直没哭，接过快餐面的孙海良哭了。“她来的时候满头黑发，刚才一低头，头顶已经有碗大的一圈白发了。”

救援出的是体力，即便最累的时候，人没找到，“你也不敢看家属的眼神”。

“是我人生最积极的时候”

电焊工高友顺　杨杰 / 摄

电焊工高友顺54岁，离异，独居，脸上总是红红的，可能跟长期做电焊有关。他家里的桌子上摆着他为队里做的捞人铁钩。小时候他有个当兵梦，听说侄子当了兵，“我买了好多烟花，沿路从家里放到镇上”。

“高友顺在路上看到堵车了，他会把车停一边，自己下去指挥交通。”队友说。他不富裕，别人请客他不去，宁可在家吃泡饭。网上跟人聊天，他用摄像头拍拍四面墙，“谁还愿意跟我交朋友”？他因为投资失败欠下20多万元债，但为了救援方便，他还是凑钱买了辆车。

一次紧急打捞落水者，正在厂里上班的高友顺请了假去救援，他把衣服一脱赤身跳入水中，回来被厂里主管责备“脑子进水了”。他索性辞了工作。

他有一个女儿，不常见面。高友顺决定死后捐赠器官，女儿不愿让他签同意书，他说：“人死了被喂狗也不知道，不如捐了还能有用。”他跟女儿说，完成器官捐赠，遗体拿回后，他请女儿一把火把遗体烧了，撒在富春江里。

虽然离婚十几年了，他跟前岳父岳母还常来往。“反正我自己的父母也没了，我叫了这么多年爸爸妈妈也叫惯了。”

他父亲患有阿尔兹海默症。一个大雨天，

老人沿着河沟走，被风吹到河里淹死了。他父亲生前也走丢过，像他搜救的很多老人一样。

有一次一个老人走失，队伍找到晚上12点。第二天下起大雨，搜救队刚上山，老人却自己走下山了。看着老人满是泥水的脸、破损的衣衫，高友顺想起了自己的父亲，父亲走的那天也是一样的风和雨，不一样的是，这位老人还活着，正拿着棍子打树上的雨水。

很多队员把野狼搜救队的紧急任务群置顶，里面不允许闲聊，任务一来，紧跟着一排“收到”。队员陈小波可能是其中最积极的一个。

陈小波40岁，看上去比实际年龄年轻。他喜欢戴鸭舌帽，下巴上长期挂着一撮胡子，手臂上有辟邪文身。朋友叫他“野人”，他在队里的名号是“孤狼”。他骑着摩托车独来独往。他差不多是队友中爬山最快的一个，“我不开心就去爬山”。

“孤狼”陈小波17岁离家出走到北京游荡，没少犯错。

他现在开了家烧烤店，起名“野狼烧

烤”，店里挂着李小龙的画和他救援得过的奖章。他说：“现在是我人生最积极的时候。”

“我一开始是进队里玩儿玩儿的，觉得有点儿约束，不自在。”多救几个人以后，他的感觉不一样了，“这像份职业，现在不是玩儿，是时间和生命”。

一次晚上有救援任务，烧烤店里正忙，女友不想他走。“她不知道轻重，只知道赚钱。”以前两个人一起开店，可第二天女友不来了，二人就这样分了手。

有人失去工作，有人失去爱情，但大家都不想离开这支队伍。“除非有一天残了，帮不上忙了。”“孤狼”陈小波轻盈地跳上一棵树，摘下野果。

民间救援“大比武”

每次救援结束，“狼头”陈青伟就把参与行动的队员名字发到朋友圈。年底，他自己做了“公益爱心之家”的牌子挂在队员家门前，“毕竟没有工资，”他指着 15 面锦旗说，“我们也就这么一点点荣誉”。

副队长史荣平擅长分析信息，调查杭州女子失踪案时，他曾去现场排查监控死角。副队长朱关金开了家饭店，那是队员集会的场所，他老婆常见他半夜回来，脚在鞋里泡得发白。王仙勇和王荣平是两兄弟，两家房子盖在一起，他们家只有这两个儿子，他俩结伴去救援。陈杭出生于1997年，是队里年龄最小的，还兼职做森林消防的工作。后勤部部长袁君其外号“员外”，他人胖胖的，出钱多过出力。钟新儿是队里少有的女将，大伙儿叫她大姐，负责财务。

田间地头出了什么麻烦事，只要“野狼”一抵达，围观群众嘴里就会说着“野狼来了”，眼睛开始放光，好像事情即将得到解决。每当那种时刻，“狼头”陈青伟就能体会到一种从未有过的价值感。

教练孙海良很高兴看到这群队员“以前可能是捣蛋鬼，现在终于挺起胸”“在别人心目中的地位越来越高，更不会跌下去”。他有时在队伍里点个名，夸赞谁进步了，被表扬的人总是把头抬得很高。

“狼头”陈青伟跟妻子开玩笑，说等到

他自己80岁时可以自豪地跟孙子谈起，“爷爷那时候是个勇敢善良的人，救助了很多人”。

“野狼”的队服是迷彩服。当初买队服时队里就出现过分歧，有人不愿意花几百元买一套救援服，说平时也穿不了几次。几经协商，大家最后选择了迷彩服，队名用魔术贴贴在背后，平时干农活的时候一撕，也能穿。

队标是“狼头”半夜起床在纸上设计出来的。“我很喜欢狼，它有灵性，又有团队精神。”他在搜索引擎上找狼头，抠下来，又加上了登山杖和闪电，代表民间户外和快速出击。

有一次上山寻人，向导走得太快，“狼头”陈青伟跟丢了，手机没有信号，GPS也失联，小竹子密密麻麻望不到天。陈青伟找路时，忽然发现头上有两条竹叶青，“啪”一下飞过来。

“我拿个小木棍把蛇推到一边。”他开始着急，对讲机里没有队友的声音，他想着：“其他队员遇到蛇怎么办？”这时，天已经暗下来，他忽然觉得害怕，他怕兄弟们无法走出大山，那种恐惧甚于毒蛇和夜晚。

当对讲机终于传来熟悉的声音时，陈青伟默默流泪了，信号一个连一个，将这群人串在一起。下山后，他没对任何人提起自己的那次崩溃。

救援最幸福的时刻是把人找到。队员们一边往下撤一边说笑，“那种笑容，平时不太容易看到”。他们有时在救援现场对着江水吃泡面，有时在饭店包间庆祝胜利。窗外，富春江水平静流过，青山依旧。大家举着酒杯，面色通红，每个人都在笑。

Fuyang Civilian 110 Hotline

They are called the "Civilian 110," and they are not affiliated with any regular team.

Their new "office" is two houses next to a cemetery. Besides selling tombstones, Chen Qingwei is the boss of the team, the "Wolf Head" of the Hangzhou Fuyang Wild Wolf Public Welfare Search and Rescue Team. His house was the headquarters. It was stacked with urns for sale and rescue ropes.

Almost all the team members are from the countryside, and they include bricklayers, welders, hunters, brewers, chicken farmers, used car salesmen, air conditioner installers, owners of small supermarkets and barbecue shops, police, doctors of village clinics, and all kinds of other people, all wearing dark green team uniforms when they are looking for missing people in the mountains and rivers. They do this job at their own risk, and do not receive any money.

One of the coaches of the Wild Wolf Search and Rescue Team is Sun Hailiang. He is a member of the Ram Team, a large civilian rescue team. He helped in Nepal after it suffered from an earthquake and Mozambique after it was hit by a typhoon. The Ram Team has one thousand members worldwide, and their rescue equipment includes sonar, diving devices and a helicopter.

The Wild Wolf Team operates only in Fuyang and focuses on rescue missions in the mountainous areas around the town of Xindeng. Their equipment includes a patch-ridden lifeboat that had to be decommissioned, a self-made underwater fishing hook to reach people in the water, and a positioning device removed from the collar of a hunting dog. Their most high-tech device was a drone that was unfortunately lost when it crashed in a hilly area during a night search and rescue operation of 23 backpackers.

"When Combating Heaven and Earth, It's Best to Take Three Steps Back"

Sun Hailiang is not an adventurous person. If he thinks there is even 20 percent chance of danger to himself when rescuing someone, he will not take the risk. Every time he puts on his uniform, his internal radar that alerts him of danger is turned on. "You have to understand that you are in a crisis situation before you go try to rescue someone."

The first lesson he taught the members of "Wild Wolf Team" is how to protect themselves. "Don't combat heaven and earth. It's best to take three steps back." He told the story of three friends who were all excellent swimmers. Because they saw the gentle flow of the Jinsha River at the Hutiao Gorge, they jumped in, but almost failed to resurface. One of them nearly drowned. He used his last ounce of strength to grab onto a rock to survive. From then on, he would tremble whenever he heard the name "Jinsha River."

"Backpackers go missing usually because they couldn't see the danger, failing to consider their physical strength, or trying to complete impossible tasks." When Sun Hailiang was young, he wanted to run a small business or be in senior management of a state-owned enterprise. Now he diligently practices Tai Chi every day and goes out every weekend to relax. He also knows traditional Chinese medicine and owns a pharmacy.

In 2008, he started to get involved in nonprofit rescue missions, and became the "Wild Wolf Team" coach three years ago. He taught the team members how to use the contour map without using any geographical jargon. "The place where the contour lines are close together is a cliff, looking like a scar on a tree." He also taught them how to give first aid and use a rope to climb down cliff sides and rocks, but the most crucial lesson focuses on safety. He asked everyone never to go into water alone when trying to save someone who can't swim as that person will surely see you as their last chance and may even drag you down trying to save themselves. "We aren't doing rescue to make money, and we should be responsible for our own safety so that our family can rest assured."

Sun Hailiang had to sign a death disclaimer every time he went out with the Ram Team. He was responsible for all the consequences, and his participation has nothing to do with the team or with China. He had been involved in several international rescue missions and had encountered "familiar faces" from other countries, all of whom were alert to the dangers just as he was. "The Germans are very strict, and the sizes of their tools and boxes fit perfectly." He told of the time when rescue team members from five countries did a joint exercise. Sun Hailiang was prone to put equipment against the wall, but the Japanese team suggested that the equipment should be put on the other side in a real rescue so that it was convenient to be carried away at any time.

Right after the earthquake in Ludian County, Yunnan Province, Sun was taking the blood pressure of a victim when an aftershock suddenly came, and the victim instantly fled with the blood pressure pad still wrapped around his arm.

Sun said life in the earthquake-stricken area was challenging but rewarding. The victims would take the rescuers to their homes to eat. Even if they only drank a cup of tea in the half-collapsed rooms, the owners were very happy. Following the rescue, the Dai people filled the rescue vehicles with peanuts and glutinous rice. When the team started the vehicles to get ready to leave, the older people and children performed a Dai dance on the roadside. As they drove away, they were still dancing.

When he went to Xizang (Tibet) for a disaster relief mission, Sun Hailiang's neck was covered with hada (long pieces of silk used as a greeting gift among the Zang and Mongolian ethnic groups). Following the rescue in Nepal, the local people shook their heads at them. At first, Sun and his rescue companions were puzzled. Later, they found out that the local people shook their heads as a custom to show respect.

Sun Hailiang is 54 years old this year, and his knee bulges due to frequent climbs in the mountains. Not long ago, he was part of the rescue mission at the Poyang Lake after the flood. There was a moment when he felt that his physical strength had taken a sharp decline. "I am afraid that one day when I sign up for a rescue mission, but will be rejected because of my health."

He still remembered the first time he participated in a rescue. The missing person was a 27-year-old young man who was raised by his mother. As the rescue team searched for him in the mountains, his mother waited with instant noodles. When someone came back, she always asked, "Did you find my son?" Everyone shook their heads. She would prepare instant noodles for everyone, saying, "You've been working so hard." From the first day to the eleventh day, his mother did not cry, but Sun Hailiang, who accepted her daily instant noodles, cried. "Her hair was black when we arrived. But by the time we left, it was turning white."

"When I am involved in a rescue mission, I use all my physical strength. Even if I am exhausted and fail to find the missing person, I don't dare to look at the family members."

"This Is the Most Positive Time of My Life"

Welder Gao Youshun is 54 years old, divorced, and lives alone. His face is always red, which may be the result from long-term welding. On a table in his house is the iron hook he made to rescue people. When he was young, he dreamed of joining the army. So when he heard that his nephew had become a soldier, he was so happy that "I bought a lot of fireworks and set them off all the way from my home to the town."

"If Gao Youshun saw a traffic jam on the road, he would always pull over and get out to direct traffic," said his team member. Gao is not rich, but he would not go out to dinner even if others offered to pay, and would rather stay home and eat reheated cooked rice. Chatting with other netizens online, he would always use the camera to show his room with little furniture and said, "Who would like to make friends with me?" He owed more than 200,000 yuan in debt because of his poor investment, but he still borrowed money to buy a car for the convenience of rescue.

One day, Gao was working in a factory, but had to ask leave to rescue someone who had fallen in the water. He took off his clothes and jumped in the water, and he rescued the person. When he came back, the factory manager said he was "out of his mind." Gao quit the factory job that day.

He has a daughter, and they seldom see each other. When Gao had decided to donate his organs after his death, his daughter was unwilling to allow him to sign the consent letter. "My body might be fed to dogs after I die," he told her. "I'd rather die knowing my organs will be used somewhere." He told her that after the organ donation is completed and his body is given back, he wanted his body cremated and his ashes scattered in the Fuchun River.

Though he got divorced more than ten years ago, he still has frequent contact with his former father-in-law and mother-in-law. "My own parents are dead. I've grown accustomed to calling them Mom and Dad for many years."

His father suffered from Alzheimer's disease. During a heavy rain one day, the elderly man was walking along the river and was thrown into the water by the wind and drowned. His father had gone missing, like many of the elderly Gao helped.

There was one time when an elderly man was lost, and the team looked for him until midnight but did not find him. There was a heavy rain the next day. Just as the search and rescue team was going up the mountain for further search, the elderly man appeared, walking down by himself. Seeing the elderly man's muddy face and worn-out clothes, Gao thought of his father. On the day when his father died, there was the same wind and rain.

Many team members give top priority to the WeChat Group of the Wild Wolf Search and Rescue Team where the emergency tasks are released. Free chatting is not allowed in this group. When there is a task, they will immediately send "received." Team member Chen Xiaobo may be the most active among them.

Chen Xiaobo is 40 years old, but looks younger than his age. He usually wears a cap, has a beard, and has a tattoo on his arm meant to ward off evil spirits. Friends call him "Barbarian," and he is called "Lone Wolf" on the team. He rides a motorcycle, and always travels alone. He is probably the fastest mountain climber of the team. Sometimes he will go climb the mountain alone if he feels unhappy.

When he was just 17, "Lone Wolf" Chen Xiaobo ran away from home to Beijing, and has made many mistakes in his life. Now he has a barbecue restaurant named "Wild Wolf BBQ." A picture of Bruce Lee is hung in the restaurant, along with medals awarded to him for his rescue work. "This is the most positive time of my life," he said.

"In the beginning, when I joined the team, I didn't take it seriously. And I felt a little restrained and uncomfortable." After rescuing a few more people, he felt different. "Rescue work is not fun. It is like a career. It's not a game. It means time and life."

Once there was a rescue task at night, but business at his barbecue restaurant was brisk and his girlfriend did not want him to go. "She was not clear about the importance of my rescue work; she only cares about making money." The next day, his girlfriend did not come to their restaurant, and they parted.

Some team members have lost their jobs, others have lost their lovers, but no one wants to leave the team. "I won't give up rescue unless I am disabled one day," Lone Wolf Chen Xiaobo said while jumping onto a tree and plucking a wild fruit.

"Great Competition" of Civilian Rescue

Every time a rescue task finishes, "Wolf Head" Chen Qingwei posts the team members' names who participated in the rescue on his WeChat Moments (a social media app timeline which everyone can see). At the end of this year, he made plates to be hung up on the doors of the team members' homes. "After all, no salaries are paid to us," he said while pointing to 15 silk banners. "We only have this honor."

Deputy Team Leader Shi Rongping is good at analyzing information. When investigating the case of a missing Hangzhou woman, he went to the scene to examine the blind angle under CCTV cameras around her living residence.

Deputy Team Leader Zhu Guanjin operates a restaurant where the team members often gather. He often returns home very late after rescue, and his wife sees his wrinkled feet due to soaking in water for a long time.

Wang Xianyong and Wang Rongping are two brothers, and are the only children of their parents. Their two houses are close, and they go on rescue missions together.

Born in 1997, Chen Hang is the youngest on the team. He has a part-time job fighting forest fires.

Yuan Junqi, the head of the team's logistics department, is nicknamed "Wealthy Gentleman." He is overweight and mainly contributes to the team through financial support.

Zhong Xin'er is a female team member, which is rare for rescue teams. Everyone calls her "elder sister," and she is in charge of finance.

If there is trouble in the field, onlookers will see the "Wild Wolf Team" arriving and say "the Wild Wolf Team is coming," and their eyes will shine brightly, knowing that the problem is about to be resolved. When that happens, "Wolf Head" Chen Qingwei experiences a sense of self-worth.

Sun Hailiang is very happy to see that the team members "may have been troublemakers before, but now they have something to be proud of. They're aware of their importance in the eyes of others." Sometimes during meetings he will praise a team member who has made great progress, and that team member will proudly raise his head high.

"Wolf Head" Chen Qingwei said that when he was 80 years old, he would proudly tell his grandson, "Grandpa was once a brave and kind person, and I've rescued many people."

The uniforms of the "Wild Wolf Team" are in a camouflage style. There were disagreements when they were buying the uniforms. Some did not want to spend the several hundred yuan, complaining that it was too much to spend on clothing they wouldn't wear that often. But finally, everyone agreed. The team name is affixed to the back with velcro which can be removed so that the clothes can still be worn during normal times when they are not on rescue missions.

Chen Qingwei designed the team logo. "I like wolves very much. They are smart and work together as a team." He got online and searched for wolf head designs on the internet, downloaded one, and added a mountain climbing stick and lightning strike to represent their team—civilian outdoor and rapid rescue.

During one mission, the team climbed a mountain in search of missing people, but their guide was travelling too fast. "Wolf Head" Chen Qingwei got lost, his mobile phone had no signal, the GPS didn't function, and the bamboo was so dense that he couldn't even see the sky. While looking for the way, he came across two poisonous green bamboo snakes hanging in the branches over his head.

After using a small wooden stick to push the snakes aside, he began to get worried. There had been no contact from his team members on the walkie-talkie, and he worried they would not know what to do if they also encountered snakes. The sky was dark, and he suddenly felt afraid that they would not be able to find their way off the mountain.

Suddenly, the walkie-talkie finally transmitted a familiar voice, and Chen Qingwei cried silently. Slowly, the signal got better, and the voices came in one by one, linking the team members. After finally arriving back at the base, he did not mention his frustration to anyone.

The happiest moment during a rescue mission is when the missing people are found. The team members joked and smiled as they returned. "They smile in a way only a rescuer can understand." Sometimes they'll eat instant noodles by a river after a rescue, and this time they celebrated their victory at a private room in a restaurant.

Outside the window of the restaurant where they celebrated their rescue victory, the Fuchun River flowed quietly, and the green mountain towered over the river. Everyone held their wine glasses, their faces flushed, and everyone was smiling.

青春经战“疫”更辉煌

The Youth's Fight Against COVID-19

作者：胡 宁
翻译：范逊敏

青春经战“疫”更辉煌

在抗击新冠肺炎疫情的战斗中，80后、90后乃至00后登上舞台，组成青年群体战“疫”的完整光谱。

在全国抗击新冠肺炎疫情先进个人表彰的青年志愿者中，汪勇是一名85后“快递小哥”，他带领其他志愿者一起为解决武汉金银潭医院职工出行、就餐等问题而努力，筑起一道“后勤保障线”。艾泽铭是北华大学大四学生，他响应共青团吉林省委的青年防疫志愿者招募，顶着寒风在长春火车站、机场、老旧小区等地进行测温、消杀、登记等志愿服务，服务83天，没有缺勤过一天。

尽管他们不是这个社会最强壮、“最有本事”的群体，但是他们年轻，他们拥有无畏、青春和热望，以及挺身而出时所展现出的强大爆发力，这些都足以为困境中的人带来生机和希望。

从一份“冲动”开始

当被问起最初做志愿者的动机时，汪勇用了两个字：冲动。

“如果极其理智地衡量得失，就没有人愿意去做志愿者了。”汪勇的判断基于这样的背景：他的家中有老人、妻子和两岁的孩子，他是全家的主要劳动力，房贷没还完，而那时的武汉，谁也说不清楚疫情会发展成什么样子。

他的这份激情与其说是冲动，不如说是无法置身事外的热血。这驱使着送了一整年快递、因疫情而提前放假的汪勇，瞒着家人成为了运送医护人员的司机、协调员和后勤保障者。

他成为志愿者的起点是2020年1月24日晚上，他在朋友圈看到一位武汉金银潭医院护士的求助：“我们这里限行了，没有公交车和地铁，回不了家，走回去要4个小时。”犹豫很久后，汪勇对妻子说：“网点临时需要值班人员，我被派去值班了。”

他打通了护士的电话，告知对方自己

只有一个N95口罩，并询问能不能给他带点酒精。护士愣住了，没想到会有人接这个单。那时，距这位护士发出求助信息已过去5个多小时了。

从这一单开始，第二单、第三单，第二天、第三天……直到武汉解封，公共交通恢复，汪勇“摆渡者”的身份才算结束。其中有一个月，他一直睡在仓库里，常常从早上忙到下午3点都没空吃一口东西。

“（那时候）活着就是天大的好处了。”汪勇衡量着自己在外奔波的意义，这笔账他是这么算的：如果每天送30名医护人员，帮他们节约60小时的通勤时间，这60小时就可以救很多很多人的命。

被这份内心的“冲动”驱使的还有很多人，比如驱车直奔武汉的湖南人郑能量、原本就从事救援队或社工服务多年的北京市红十字雷锋车队应急救援志愿服务队队长李峰威、山西天龙救援队队长陆玫、累计卸载货物50多吨的荆门市益动社工服务中心负责人王丽莉，以及受到表彰的防疫志愿者中唯一一位在校大学生——艾泽铭。

无法旁观的艾泽铭经历了83天忙碌的日子。这名1998年出生的医学生每天看着感染人数在增长“心里着急”。“这次大家都是有十分力恨不得拿出十五分来”，由于太过出力，他还曾被强制要求休息。

“作为医学生，本身就觉得自己有这份责任，只是我水平还不到可以去武汉的程度。”大年初二，艾泽铭看到了共青团吉林省委招募青年防疫志愿者的通知后，第一时间报了名。

一开始，他被安排做线上科普宣传工作。2020年2月4日，他正式到防疫一线——长春火车站，协助车站工作人员进行测体温及对异常旅客的处置工作。那天也是艾泽铭的22岁生日。前一天，他刚刚签下了遗体器官捐赠的协议，注册成为一名人体器官捐献志愿者，承诺如遇不幸要将自己的器官、遗体捐赠给有需要的人。

在艾泽铭心里，做志愿者虽有一定危险，但是害怕、担忧这些情绪并没有太多困扰到他。在他看来一切自然而然，“我入学的时候是宣过誓的，作为医学生，这些都是我该做的。”

做志愿者不能仅凭一腔热血

几乎所有志愿者回顾战“疫”经历时都认同一件事：做志愿者不能仅凭一腔热血，内心有冲动才站出来，但是冲动并不等于莽撞。

汪勇做志愿者的时候每天跟医护人员长时间待在一起，这让他比外界更清楚他们需要什么。有人吃够了泡面、面包，就想念米饭的香气。有人觉得叫车太慢，想骑共享电动车快点儿回去休息。有人要修眼镜，买拖鞋、指甲钳、充电器甚至秋衣秋裤，等等，这些过去随手就能解决的问题在特殊时期的武汉都变成了难题。

汪勇做不到大包大揽，无法一个人解决一切。他被这些需求驱动着，从一个没什么社会资源的快递小哥，变成要跟企业、店商、政府部门沟通的协调者。医护人员们想吃米饭，他就要找餐厅；餐厅的仓库被迫要关闭，他就去找有关部门说明情况。最有成就感的一次是，他得知金银潭医院的医护人员需要电动车出行，他就去找共享电动车公司协调，最后公司在金银潭医院周围投放了400辆共享电动车，别的医院的人都很羡慕，他又去帮助别的医院一并协调资源。经他协调，滴滴公司还把相关医院接单的公里数从3.5公里以内更改为15公里以内，需要打车回家的医护人员有更多的车可约叫。

很多事情“超乎我的认识”，汪勇说。他没想到微信朋友圈和志愿者的互助合作能迸发出这么大的能量，资源一旦对接成功，让专业的人做专业的事，很多困难就迎刃而解了。

汪勇也在志愿行动过程中习得了另一种“专业性”——学会给自己画“红线”。为了保证自己接送的医护人员的安全，他给自己立了规矩：不管在路上看到多可怜的陌生人，他都要狠下心不能拉；不能进到医院里，唯一一次破例进医院，还是因为一个老人不吃心脏病药会有性命之忧。

做到这一点并不容易。那时的武汉整个城市是空空荡荡的，汪勇开着车走在街道上，最期待的就是迎面能遇上一辆车，“那种空虚和害怕是言语表达不了的”。他每次经过大桥时几乎都会看到骑车过桥骑到一半没力气的人，每次看到他心里都很难受，想停下来载人走，但是他不能——他要保证医护人员不会因他而交叉感染。

还有一些志愿者，他们是专业的社会工作者，比如专业的心理咨询师，专业本身就是他们最好的武器。

艾泽铭也属于这类，医学本身就是他的专业。有医学知识的他对消毒、防护等操作规程接受速度更快、防护意识更强。从心理到体力的准备，他都比很多非医学专业的人更为充分。

在长春火车站服务期间，每天晚上艾泽铭十点休息，第二天凌晨两点多起床，下碗面，配着妈妈留给他的酱料吃。他说，这样是为了给胃排空留足时间，以免穿上防护服后想去洗手间。近20天的时间里，他几乎每天只吃一顿正常的饭，上岗前从不喝水，每天最早到岗。

零下20多摄氏度的长春火车站外，他穿着防护服经历“冰火两重天”：防护服覆盖的部分因为热而有水汽，带着薄薄的医用手套的手又冻得伸不直，头发尖儿上还挂着冰碴儿。他不停地搓手、跺脚，让自己在东北冰天雪地的户外能保暖。

在火车站服务期间，他担任青年防疫志愿者服务队团支书，先后带领4批志愿者不间断地开展志愿服务，团队累计为旅客测温28.9万人次，服务时长为2455小时，上报并妥善安排体温异常旅客数百人。其中一位去过武汉的大哥几次测量体温都过高，艾泽铭当时也没觉得紧张。他比普通人更有医学知识，这让他面对疫情时更具平常心。利用自己的经验，艾泽铭累计为300多名即将上岗的志愿者进行了辅导。

“这份荣誉不是给我一个人的”

这段战“疫”经历，是很多志愿者平

淡生活中的高光时刻。

这份“高光”给了一些人以新的机会。比如汪勇，他从一个快递员变成了分部经理，升职了，也有了更大的责任。他琢磨着怎么能让自己的工作伙伴也愉快地获得更多收入。以前他从没想过自己有机会参与、策划顺丰公益基金会为抗“疫”临时成立的公益项目，免费为支援湖北的医护人员寄行李，为1000户孤寡老人每个月持续送关爱包直到第二年。

最初做志愿者时，汪勇觉得东拼西凑10万元都很困难。但是后来，他入党了，获得了“中国青年五四奖章”，上了新闻联播，很多人因为他的事迹捐数百万元物资给定点医院，这是他以前想都不敢想的事儿。

艾泽铭在学校时是生活班长，但是他觉得自己有点“社交恐惧症”，只是在别人需要帮忙时，这份“热心肠”才能让他突破“社恐”。做青年防疫志愿者的日子里，他要快速跟一大批陌生人熟悉并共同作战，每天要跟成千上万名陌生旅客、小区居民主动沟通。这个觉得自己不算勤快的男孩儿自己感觉“当时走路都带风”。

85后汪勇和95后艾泽铭，这两位青年防疫志愿者都提到了社会曾经给他们贴上的标签：“垮掉的一代”“任性”“心理脆弱”“不靠谱”……但是这些标签对于他们完全不适用。

汪勇接送过00后的“小丫头片子”。这位小护士连充电器都没带、什么情况都不知道就回医院进行支援。类似的小事促使他坚持做志愿者。传递温暖在他看来是一种责任。获得荣誉了，也意味着他身上的责任变大了。

疫情期间汪勇脸上瘦出来的棱角如今又圆了回来。5月，汪勇带着妻子孩子迎来了疫情暴发后的第一次放松。他在游乐园看着孩子们奔跑在阳光下，突然有点感慨，“幸福原来这么简单”。

疫情让武汉“伤了些元气”，但是汪勇觉得，靠着一个个普通人的努力，时间会让武汉人慢慢消化伤痛。

吉林舒兰聚集性疫情暴发后，艾泽铭

主动到长春市富城社区万星幸福城小区报到，上午上网课，下午做志愿服务。每当社区有外来或体温异常人员进入，他都得第一时间上前接触、排查、登记，没有一天让人替班。

荣誉随之而来，但是艾泽铭也感受到了压力。“这些不是属于我一个人的，我只是志愿者中的一个。”在这次战“疫”过程中，他感受到付出赋予他新的力量，让他想深入了解如何做更专业的志愿者。

有一件事被艾泽铭写进了自己的战“疫”日记。2020年2月11日，他在长春火车站测温，一个看起来只有四五岁的小孩儿红外测温显示异常，他安安静静地在旁边摘了帽子等待二次测温。二次测量正常后，孩子顺利进站。走了几步后孩子突然停下，转回身直直地看着艾泽铭的眼睛，冲他鞠了个躬。

The Youth's Fight Against COVID-19

In the battle against COVID-19, young people in their 20s, 30s and 40s are showing their abilities by joining groups to fight the epidemic.

Wang Yong is a delivery courier in his 30s, but he also worked as a volunteer providing transportation and meals for the staff of Wuhan Jinyintan Hospital. This earned him the award "National Advanced Individual in the Fight Against COVID-19."

Ai Zeming, a senior at Beihua University, was recruited by the Communist Youth League of the Jilin Provincial Party Committee to help with epidemic prevention work. For 83 consecutive days in the cold weather, he was stationed at the Changchun Railway Station, the airport, and communities where he checked people's temperatures and helped with disinfection and registration.

Although they are not the strongest or "most capable" group in society, their youth, fearlessness and passion brought them to the forefront of the COVID-19 battle, and helped provide hope to those who needed it.

Starting with an Impulse

When asked about his initial motivation to be a volunteer, Wang Yong said one word: impulse.

“If all you care about are gains and losses, you can never be a volunteer.” Wang is the breadwinner of his family. He has to support his wife, two-year-old child and elderly parents. He also has to pay his mortgage. Despite this, he still made his decision to be a volunteer. At that time, no one in Wuhan knew what the future would be, including him.

His decision to help was not driven so much by passion, but by the impulse that he did not want to just stand by doing nothing. Without telling his family, Wang Yong – who had been a delivery courier for a year and had an early holiday due to the epidemic —was suddenly motivated to become the driver, coordinator, and logistics provider for medical workers in the city.

He began volunteering on January 24, 2020 after he saw a nurse from Wuhan Jinyintan Hospital posting a message on her social media WeChat Moments asking for help. “Buses and subways are suspended near my hospital. I can’t go home. It would take me four hours to walk home. ” After hesitating for a long time, Wang Yong finally decided to act, but he had to lie to his wife in case she wouldn’t allow him to go. “The branch office needs someone on duty now, and I was assigned,” he told her.

He then called the nurse to take her home, but he lacked the proper prevention materials. He only had one N95 mask and asked if the nurse could bring him some disinfectant. The nurse was surprised to hear from him. By then, it had been over five hours since the nurse had sent her message for help.

From this order, the second order, the third order, every day comes new order... It wasn't until Wuhan's lockdown ended and public transport resumed that Wang Yong stopped this work. He slept in a warehouse for that month, and was often too busy working to eat anything from morning until 3 pm.

"At that time, I was just happy to be alive." Wang Yong explained his actions this way: if he could transport 30 medical workers to and from work every day, it could save 60 hours of their travel time. They could then use those 60 hours to save more lives.

Many volunteers were also driven by such passion, like Zheng Nengliang, driving straight to Wuhan from his hometown in Hunan; Li Fengwei, the leader of the emergency rescue team of the Beijing Red Cross volunteer service who has been engaged in a rescue and social work team for many years; Lu Mei, the head of the Shanxi Dragon Rescue Team; Wang Lili, director of the social work service center in Jingmen who helped with the logistics of more than 50 tons of goods; and Ai Zeming, the only college student of all the epidemic prevention volunteers to receive an award.

Medical school student Ai Zeming was born in 1988. He joined the group to fight the COVID-19 epidemic, and was busy working for 83 days. At that time, he became worried seeing the rising number of infections every day. "During this period of time, we have to do beyond our best." Others had to force him to rest because he was working too hard.

"As a medical student, I felt it was my duty to help, but my skills were not good enough to volunteer in Wuhan." On the second day of the

Chinese New Year, Ai noticed that the Communist Youth League of Jilin Provincial Committee was recruiting young volunteers to help in epidemic prevention work. He immediately volunteered.

At first, he was assigned to be an online influencer. On February 4, 2020, he was transferred to Changchun Railway Station, the frontline of epidemic prevention, to assist the station staff in checking temperatures and take care of people with high temperatures. That was his 22nd birthday. The day before, he had registered as an organ donor, promising to donate his organs and body to those in need after his death.

Although volunteering is dangerous work during an epidemic, Ai was not scared or did not worry. "I took an oath when I started medical school. As a medical student, that's what I'm supposed to do."

Volunteers Need to Be Well-Prepared

Almost every volunteer said the same exact words when they recalled their experience fighting the epidemic: being a volunteer demands more than passion and impulsiveness. You need to be well-prepared.

At that time, Wang spent most of his time with the medical workers, which gave him a better idea of what they needed. Some people ate a lot of instant noodles and bread and wanted some rice and other dishes. Some people thought it took a long time to hail a ride and wanted to ride the shared electric scooters to go home quickly. Some people needed to have their glasses repaired or buy slippers, nail clippers, chargers, and even thermal underwear. All of these things were once readily available, but had become difficult to get in Wuhan during that particular period.

Although Wang could not solve everything by himself, he remembered all these demands and tried to find the solutions. As a courier, he had few resources, but gradually he became the coordinator who communicated with enterprises, shopkeepers and government departments. When the medics wanted rice, he went to the restaurants. When the restaurant warehouses were forced to close, he went to the related government departments to explain what they needed. When he learned that the medical workers in Jinyintan Hospital needed electric bikes, he coordinated with the electric bike-sharing company who agreed to provide 400 electric bikes around Jinyintan Hospital. People in other hospitals also asked for his help, so he coordinated with the company for more electric bikes. He also talked to ride-hailing app Didi to change the distance from within 3.5 kilometers to within 15 kilometers around some hospitals so that more cars would be available for medical workers. According to Wang Yong, this was one of the most rewarding experiences.

“Lots of things were beyond my understanding,” Wang Yong said. He did not expect that so many people would respond to calls for mutual help and cooperation on the WeChat Moments. Once he was able to connect all the professionals or related departments, many difficulties got solved quickly.

Wang also learned another “skill” in his work knowing when to draw the line. To ensure the safety of the medical workers he transported, he made a rule: he would never pick up people on the way to the hospital, no matter how sick or how poor they looked. The only exception was one elderly man he picked up who was in danger of dying if he did not receive heart medicine.

It was not easy to keep this rule. At that time, Wuhan was an empty city. Driving on the streets, he looked forward to seeing other cars. "Words can't express the feelings of emptiness and fear," he recalled. Every time he passed the Wuhan Yangtze River Bridge, he would see someone on a bike crossing the bridge but with no energy to go any further. Every time he saw this, he felt sad and wanted to stop and help, but he couldn't, he had to make sure that the medical workers wouldn't get infected.

Other volunteers are social workers, such as psychological counselors, who use their professional abilities to help others.

Ai Zeming, who majored in medicine, was a professional medical volunteer. He knew disinfection, protection and other operating procedures, and he understood what to do and how to do it more efficiently. When he worked, he had a stronger awareness of protection. He was better prepared both mentally and physically than other non-medical volunteers.

While serving at Changchun Railway Station, Ai would go to bed at 10 pm and get up around 2 am. Early in the morning, he would eat a bowl of noodles, with the sauce prepared by his mother. He said that this allowed him enough time to use the bathroom in the morning so that he wouldn't need to take off his protective suit later during the day. For nearly 20 days, he only ate one meal a day and never drank water before work. He was always the first to arrive those days.

Standing outside Changchun Railway Station, with temperatures below -20°C, Ai would wear a protective suit to endure the extreme weather. In the suit, his body would produce heat and moisture, which would later turn to ice, and would freeze his hands in his thin medical gloves. Ice would form on the ends of his hair. He would rub his hands and stomp his feet to stay warm in the icy weather of northeast China.

He served as the branch secretary of the Youth Epidemic Prevention Volunteer Service Team at the railway station. He led four groups of volunteers to carry out services continuously. The team took the temperatures of around 289,000 passengers and served over 2,455 hours. Hundreds of passengers with high temperatures were reported and adequately helped. Ai once met a middle-aged man who had been to Wuhan. Though the man's temperature was high after several checks, Ai was not worried. Because he had more medical knowledge, he felt calmer in the face of the epidemic. Ai also tutored more than 300 volunteers who had also come to help.

The Awards Belong to All Volunteers

Many volunteers regard this experience as one of the most unforgettable times of their life.

This experience has allowed some people to discover new abilities within themselves. Wang Yong, for example, was promoted from being a delivery man to a division manager. With more responsibilities, he began to think about how to help his workers earn more money. He never thought that he would have the opportunity to plan and participate in a temporary public welfare project organized by the SF Foundation to fight the epidemic. It was a program that delivered personal packages for free for the medical workers in Hubei and would also send care packages to 1,000 senior citizens who did not have families.

Early in his volunteering, Wang found it very difficult to raise even 100,000 yuan for the foundation. But later, after he became a member of the Communist Party of China and won the "May 4th Medal for Chinese Youth" and his story was reported on CCTV news, many people began donating millions of yuan to designated hospitals.

Though Ai Zeming had been the class monitor in school, he admitted he had some social anxiety. Only when others needed his help could he overcome his social phobia. As an epidemic prevention volunteer, he quickly got familiar with many other volunteers that he never met before and then worked with them. Every day, he talked to thousands of travelers and residents in the community. Ai did not consider himself a diligent person in daily life, but while doing the volunteer work, he said he was so busy that he "moved as fast as the wind" every day.

Wang Yong and Ai Zeming both said they had experienced some generational bias against them. Someone labeled them the "Beat Generation, capricious, fragile, and unreliable." After their hard work, however, they have proven those people wrong.

Wang once picked up a young nurse who had just turned 20, even younger than him. The young nurse was in such a hurry to support the hospital that she had no time to take her phone charger or take time to know what the situation was like. People like her inspired Wang to continue his volunteer work. He saw it as a duty to help and give warmth to more people. He said that after receiving the award, he felt a greater responsibility to help others.

During the epidemic, Wang g lost a lot of weight due to the hard work, but since then he has gained back the weight. In May, Wang and his wife finally found time to relax. It was the first time they had taken their son to the amusement park since the epidemic broke out. Wang said that seeing all the children running in the sun, he felt that "happiness lies in the simple things."

Though Wuhan had shut down during the epidemic, Wang believed that with the efforts or ordinary people, the city would come alive again and time would heal all wounds.

After the outbreak in the city of Shulan in Jilin, Ai Zeming applied to work at the Fucheng Community in Changchun. He took online classes in the morning and volunteered in the afternoon. Whenever there were outsiders or people with high temperatures who came to the community, he checked and registered them immediately. He never missed a day of work.

Ai felt a lot of pressure after he received the award. "The award is not just for me. It is for all volunteers, and I'm just one of them." During the fight against the epidemic, he felt that his dedication had given him new strength, and made him want to learn more about how to be a professional volunteer.

In his diary, Ai Zeming wrote about fighting the epidemic, and noted one thing in particular. On February 11, 2020, when he was taking temperatures at Changchun Railway Station, a child around 4 or 5 years old had a high temperature shown on the infrared thermometer. The boy quietly took off his hat and Ai took his temperature again. After making sure his temperature was normal, the boy went into the station. After taking a few steps, the boy stopped, turned around, looked Ai Zeiming straight in the eye, and bowed to him.

从白血病患者到公益基金发起人

From Leukemia to a Welfare Fund Founder

作者：桂　杰
翻译：薛彧威

从白血病患者到公益基金发起人

徐亚飞总是微笑着。她递上来的名片上赫然写着“中华慈善总会亚飞公益基金发起人、中华志愿者协会爱心企业家”等名头，而“北京东方亿轩商贸有限公司董事长”这个名头则放到了最后一行。

2018年3月26日，中华慈善总会亚飞公益基金启动仪式在全国政协礼堂举行。在启动仪式上，徐亚飞向中华慈善总会捐赠2000万元。该基金主要面向困境中的社会弱势群体对他们开展教育、健康、技能、扶贫等方面的慈善项目和活动，尤其致力于爱心图书室、心理辅导、技能培训等关爱青少年方面的慈善项目和活动。

“谢谢各位领导、朋友们百忙之中来参加成立仪式。”捐赠当天上午，徐亚飞一开口，嗓音是沙哑的。中华慈善总会副会长张倩玉说：“对于亚飞公益基金成立的事情，她事无巨细，全心投入其中，要不是她自己说，我根本不相信她是正在康复的白血病患者。几天前，北京气温下降，她着凉了，还在吐血，我看了真心疼。”

从企业家到从事公益事业，徐亚飞走过了一段不为人知的崎岖的伤病之路。

“原来死神离我这么近”

徐亚飞是一位70后创业者，来自“中国慈孝文化之乡”浙江省慈溪市。20岁时，徐亚飞只身来到北京创业，通过专注旱冰鞋销售改变了命运。徐亚飞2005年开始涉足服装行业，2010年开启自主品牌服饰的生产和销售。然而，就在事业如日中天的时候，不幸却降临了。

2013年8月23日，徐亚飞被告知患上了慢粒白血病，接着就是5个月的住院、化疗。“我一直觉得自己的病不严重，开始的时候进行保守治疗。直到2014年春节转院到天津血液病医院，医院先后几次下达病危通知书，我那时才觉得，原来死神离我这么近。”

在漫长的治疗和病痛的折磨中，徐亚飞

曾一度陷入迷茫和绝望，甚至在化疗期间为自己安排好了后事。为了不让年幼的女儿过于悲伤，徐亚飞在给女儿的绝笔信中这样写道："妈妈走后，轩轩你要听话，要坚强，长大一定要记住那些帮助过我们母女俩的好心人的恩情，妈妈留给你的30多份光盘录音和199封信，你一定要按照妈妈的吩咐一一听完、读完，并亲自交给妈妈所交代的每一位叔叔和阿姨……轩轩，妈妈昨天告诉丁老师'五一'想让你来医院陪我几天，其实妈妈是想带你去一个好地方，妈妈想让你在那里等我6年。你这6年里先不要见我，更不要找我，因为妈妈在医院治病是不能见任何人的，等你16岁的时候就可以见到妈妈了。"

而当时刚满10岁的女儿得知妈妈患上白血病后，在一篇题为《我的妈妈》的作文中这样写道："班里的同学都说我的妈妈去天堂了，都说我是个没爸没妈的孩子，我每次听到这话就会哭。表妹艺婷告诉我，我的妈妈得的是白血病。寒假我要去医院陪妈妈，每天从小窗口为妈妈送粥，护士阿姨说我的妈妈很坚强。我要在网上查治疗白血病的药，用我存钱罐里的钱和卖出我的画的钱给妈妈买药。妈妈，等你病好了，你可以每天陪在我身边，我们可以幸福快乐地在一起。这就是我的妈妈，我有一个世界上最好的妈妈，我爱我的妈妈。”

“我一直留着齐腰的长发，化疗打针，每天早上枕头上一把一把的全是脱落的头发，我对着镜子哭，特别崩溃。”徐亚飞不掩饰自己曾经的痛苦，她手机里保留着病床上的光头照，“我那时非常无助，唯一的寄托在骨髓捐赠上，但又不知道自己有没有那么幸运。”

这是她此生得到的来自社会的最大回报和帮助

“白血病骨髓移植首先可以考虑亲人。我父亲患有癌症，苦苦支撑多年，最后去世，母亲身体不好，唯一的哥哥抽烟喝酒血液不符合要求。我们只好借助中华骨髓库向外寻找。”徐亚飞说。

病床上的徐亚飞在忐忑不安和焦虑中度

过每一分每一秒，她能感觉到自己的无助，写给女儿的遗书堆满了一个鞋盒。她还录制了一个视频，希望在葬礼的时候播放，向所有的人做最后的告别。对于死亡，她已经做好了准备。有一次，她昏睡了5天5夜，想到孩子，才终于从病魔中醒来。

真爱感动上苍。2015年1月26日，一位来自河南农村的捐赠者的骨髓与徐亚飞的骨髓配对成功，相合指数高达8个点。这位没有成家的农村小伙子用自己的骨髓救助了素不相识的徐亚飞。“我太感动了，没想到这种幸运居然能够降临到自己身上，我曾经觉得自己已经没有生的机会了，没有想到又活了过来。”谈到接受骨髓捐赠，徐亚非至今感动不已，她认为这是她此生得到的来自社会的最大回报和帮助。

一道生的光芒把徐亚飞从黑暗中托举出来，她未曾想到过会拥有这束光的温暖和力量。

2015年4月手术之后，徐亚飞的身体极其虚弱，在床上躺了50多天下不了床，几乎连喝水的力气都没有。此时，很多朋友通过微信、电话、写卡片等各种方式鼓励她，祝愿她能够早日康复，说“女强人不要倒下”。乖巧懂事的女儿也来到医院，每天通过无菌舱的窗口为她送粥，并呼唤着“妈妈，妈妈”。

徐亚飞说：“当时，我许下两个心愿——一是康复后出院带女儿去天安门广场真正看一次升国旗，和女儿拍一张合影，圆她一个美丽的梦想；二就是一定要做公益反哺社会，在自己的余生尽力去帮助他人。”

“妹妹做公益的提议我肯定支持”

在医院治疗的时间里，徐亚飞见到很多只有两三岁的孩子，有的因为费用不得不放弃治疗，有的因为无法治疗而走向生命终点。“我想用我的能力去帮助那些需要帮助的人。”徐亚飞说。

治疗白血病是一个漫长的过程，4年多的治疗，已经让她精疲力竭、倾家荡产。为了把这份关爱传递下去，她决定在康复期间，携手团队开启自己的二次创业。在家人和朋友的大力支持下，徐亚飞自筹资金，于2017年4月22日注册北京东方亿轩商贸有限公司，主营职业服装。同年9月，在慈溪市环杭州湾创新中心创办宁波东方亿轩服饰有限公司，创新开发功能型职业装——智能健康类服饰穿戴产品。

徐亚飞的哥哥徐荣杰也是亚飞公益基金的理事，不管是作为亲人还是作为创业伙伴，徐荣杰总是选择和妹妹坚定地站在一起。“2017年在北京成立公司的时候妹妹就对我说，哥哥，我想把公司利润的5%～10%拿出来做公益，你支持吗？”

徐荣杰告诉记者，在很多人看来，妹妹徐亚飞简直是在胡闹，医治父亲的癌症及妹妹的白血病让家里的经济条件变得不容乐观，挣了钱不自己改善生活还要去做慈善，简直不可思议。他说：“父母从小就教育我们兄妹两个，忠厚传家，与人为善，妹妹做公益的提议我肯定支持。”

令徐家兄妹俩没想到的是，他们做公益的想法还得到一些朋友的支持。浙江省慈溪市戴家路村的村支书，多年的合作伙伴、苹果服装的负责人，还有北京一家投资公司的朋友，他们都从自己的企业中拿出资金投入亚飞公益基金，义无反顾地支持亚飞的事业。

正在艰难度过排异期的徐亚飞说到自己的公益基金脸上都是笑容。她说："我从小特别爱笑，外出打拼，什么样的困难都拦不住我，我笑一笑就过去了；生病的时候，我是边哭边笑，哭是真的，笑是假的；现在做公益，我的笑容是发自心底的。"

2018年1月25日，徐亚飞在她生病后第一次坐飞机，以亚飞公益基金的名义为贵州省黔西南布依族苗族自治州普安县保冲小学捐赠10万元，还为孩子们购置了大量的文具、书包等物品。"飞机落地后，又走了4个小时的山路，当天就反应很大，整个人都水肿了。"但在捐赠仪式上，徐亚飞笑得和花儿一样，外人一点都看不出她的病痛。

2018年春节前，亚飞和哥哥又赶到慈溪市社会福利院，为那里的100多位老人送去红色的羊绒围巾、保温水杯和福字。紧接着，他们又到天圆镇去看望那里80岁以上的137位老人，送去色拉油和五常大米。

"我懂得做公益不是一件容易的事情，我们兄妹愿意边学边做，以自己微薄的力量去回报社会。"徐荣杰说。

From Leukemia to a Welfare Fund Founder

Xu Yafei loves smiling. On her business card, such titles as Founder of Yafei Public Welfare Fund under the China Charity Federation and Caring Entrepreneur of China Volunteers Association are quite eye-catching, while Chairwoman of Beijing Dongfangyixuan Business and Trade Co., Ltd. is located at the bottom.

On March 26, 2018, the launch ceremony for Yafei Public Welfare Fund under the China Charity Federation was held at the Auditorium of the Chinese People's Political Consultative Conference (CPPCC) National Committee. During the ceremony, Xu made a donation of 20 million yuan (roughly USD 3 million) to the China Charity Federation. Mainly targeted at the disadvantaged groups in society, the fund would be used to carry out charitable projects and activities focusing on education, health improvement, skill training, and poverty reduction, especially those related to the caring for youngsters such as libraries, psychological counseling, and skills training.

"Thank you all for taking time out of your busy schedules to come to today's event," Xu said in a hoarse voice during the ceremony. Zhang Qianyu, Vice President of the China Charity Federation said, "She has been devoting herself heart and soul to establishing the Yafei Welfare Fund. If she hadn't told me, I would never believe that she is a patient still recovering from leukemia. A few days ago, she caught a cold due to the temperature drop in Beijing. Seeing that she was vomiting blood, I felt heartbroken."

From a businesswoman to a public welfare founder, Xu Yafei traveled down a bumpy path that was known to few people.

"I Was So Close to Death"

Xu was born in the 1970s. She came from Cixi, Zhejiang Province, a place dubbed "China's Filial Piety City." At the age of 20, she came to Beijing on her own and started a business by selling roller skates. The business was a success. In 2005, she set foot in the clothing industry and began the production and sale of her self-made brand five years later. Unfortunately, ill luck befell the woman when she was at the apex of her career.

On August 23, 2013, Xu was informed that she had contracted chronic granulocytic leukemia. In the following five months, she was in hospital receiving chemotherapy. "I have always thought that my condition wasn't so serious and only needed conservative treatments in the beginning. During the Spring Festival of 2014, I was transferred to the Hospital of Blood Diseases in Tianjin where I got several critical condition notices. Only then did I realize that I was so close to death!"

The endless treating process and sufferings once plunged Xu into confusion and desperation. She even planned for what happened after she died during the chemotherapy period. To comfort her young daughter, she wrote a letter to her, “Xuanxuan, after Mom leaves, be a good girl with a strong will. After you grow up, don’t ever forget the kind people who helped us. I will give you more than 30 CD recordings and 199 letters. Please remember my words — after listening to all the recordings and reading all the letters, you should hand them in person to every aunt and uncle whose names are written down.... Xuanxuan, yesterday I told your teacher, Ms. Ding, that I’d like to have you come to the hospital and stay with me during the May Day holiday. In fact, I will bring you to a good place, where you can spend six years waiting for me. During that period of time, don’t meet me nor try to look for me, because I won’t be allowed to meet with anyone while receiving hospital treatment. You will see Mom as you reach 16.”

The girl, who had just turned ten years old at the time, wrote this in a composition titled “My Mother” upon learning her mom had been diagnosed with leukemia. “Many of my classmates say my mom has gone to Heaven, and that I’m a child without parents. I’d burst into tears every time I heard this. My cousin Yiting told me that Mom has leukemia. I will go to the hospital to see her during the winter vacation. Every day, I will bring her porridge through the small window. The nurses told me that my mom was brave and strong while facing the disease. I will search for medicines that cure leukemia on the internet, and use the money in my piggy bank and that I earned from selling my paintings to buy them for her. Mom, after your recovery, you can be with me every day and we will live a very happy life together. This is my mother, the best mother in the world. I love her!"

"I used to have waist length hair, but after receiving chemotherapy by injection, I could see a lot of it left on the pillow every morning. I suffered a mental breakdown and cried in front of the mirror." Yafei did not conceal the pain she had gone through, and still kept a photo of her lying on the sickbed—she was completely bald then. "At the time, I felt so helpless that I could only pin my hopes on marrow transplant. But I had no idea whether I could be lucky enough to get it."

The Greatest Reward She Ever Received from Society

"One's family members are usually considered as first-hand donors," Xu recalled. "My father had suffered from cancer for many years and died of the disease in the end, my mother was poor in health, and my sole brother's blood couldn't meet the requirements because of his smoking and drinking habits. What I could do was to seek a donor from the China Marrow Donor Program."

On her sickbed, Xu Yafei felt stressed all the time and constantly worried about everything. Overwhelmed by a sense of helplessness, she wrote a pile of letters to her daughter which could fill up a shoe box. She even recorded a video to be played at her funeral, so that she could bid farewell to everyone. The woman had prepared for death. Once in a lethargic state for five days and nights, she finally woke up thinking of her child.

True love worked miracles. On January 26, 2015, the bone marrow of a donor from Henan Province matched with that of Xu Yafei. She was saved by an unmarried young man from the countryside, who was a stranger to her. "I was deeply touched, as I had never expected such good luck could happen to me. I used to think there would be no hope for me to live any longer but was ultimately given a second life." Speaking of the marrow donation, Xu regarded it as the greatest reward and help she has ever received from society.

A ray of light lifted her out of darkness, giving her warmth and strength of life which she had never expected.

After the surgery in April 2015, Xu was so weak that she laid in bed for over 50 days. During that period of time, WeChat messages, phone calls as well as postcards flooded in from her friends, encouraging her to be strong and wishing her a speedy recovery. Her lovely daughter came to the hospital every day and brought her porridge into the aseptic ward through the window. The girl often called out, "Mom, Mom!"

Xu said, "I made two wishes at the time: firstly, after leaving the hospital, I want to take my daughter to Tiananmen Square to watch the flag-raising ceremony and take a picture with her to fulfill her long-cherished hope; secondly, I want repay society through charity and spend the rest of my life helping those in need."

"I'll Give Full Support to My Sister"

During her stay at the hospital, Xu saw many children around the age of two or three, some of whom had to give up treatment due to the high costs while others died because their conditions were beyond curing. “I want to use my abilities to help the people in need,” she said.

Curing leukemia was a long, arduous process. Four years of treatment had made Xu exhausted and cost most of her family fortune. Nonetheless, with a view to passing on the care and love, she decided to join hands with her team to start a new business. With the support of her family and friends, Xu raised funds and registered the Beijing Dongfangyixuan Business and Trade Co., Ltd. on April 22, 2017, which was mainly engaged in occupational clothing sales. In September that year, she established the Ningbo Dongfangyixuan Clothing Co., Ltd. at the Hangzhou Bay Rim Innovation Center in Cixi, Zhengjiang Province. The company has been doing R & D of functional occupational clothing — smart health clothes and wearable products.

Her elder brother, Xu Rongjie, is also a board member of the Yafei Welfare Fund. As her family and business partner, he always chooses to stand by his sister. “When she set up a company in Beijing in 2017, she asked me, ‘Brother, I plan to spend 5-10% of our profits on charity. Would you support me?’”

Xu Rongjie told the reporter that in the eyes of many people, his sister was doing something crazy: treating their father’s cancer and her disease had already drained the family fortune, so it would be incredible for them to use the money they earned in philanthropy instead of improving their own lives. He said, "We were told by our parents since childhood that we should carry forward our family tradition of honesty and tolerance, and always be ready to help others. Therefore, I give full support to my sister's proposition."

The two had never expected that their idea of doing charity would win the support of many friends, including the Party Secretary of Daijialu Village of Cixi, their old business partners, Manager of Apple Clothing, and their friend from an investment company in Beijing. All of them took money from their own business and put it into Yafei Public Welfare Fund to show their support for her undertaking.

Yafei, who was enduring the rejection period after the operation, smiled with optimism when talking about her public welfare fund. She said, "I have loved to smile ever since I was a little girl. While away from home to make a living, I wasn't daunted by any obstacles; when I was ill, I often shed tears while smiling. The tears were real, but the smile was forced; now I'm engaged in helping the public, so the smile is from the bottom of my heart."

On January 25, 2018, she took her first flight since diagnosed with the disease. In the name of Yafei Public Welfare Fund, she went to Pu'an County in Guizhou Province, donated 100,000 yuan to the Baochong Primary School there as well as a lot of stationery and schoolbags for the children. "After landing, we spent four hours on the mountain path. My reaction was so strong that day that I had edema all over my body." During the donation ceremony, however,

Yafei smiled heartily so no one could discern she was a patient.

Prior to the Spring Festival in 2018, Yafei and her brother headed to the Social Welfare Center of Cixi City, sending red cashmere scarves, thermos, and new year posters to the more than 100 seniors living there. Then they paid visits to the 137 elderly individuals over the age of 80 at Tianyuan Town and sent them salad oil and high-quality rice.

"I understand that doing public welfare is not something easy. But I, along with my younger sister, would like to go ahead with it while drawing experience, so that we can repay society with our efforts," Xu Rongjie said.

Scan for a Video

传递生命最后的礼物

The Last Presents of Life

作者：张国文
翻译：薛彧威

传递生命最后的礼物

在过去10年里，下岗工人老赵平均每个月都要送走一位死者。他随身总是装着一朵白花，以备送别之用。

67岁的赵永华已将116人的遗体抬上汽车，送进了天津医科大学的解剖楼里。他确切地知道，总有一天自己也将躺着进入那幢灰色建筑物，成为学生们解剖刀下的对象，人们会在胸前戴上一模一样的白花来送他。届时，老赵的双眼里那层透明的角膜首先会被取下，拯救两位失明者。他扒开自己的眼角，比画着说，“一个人，给俩人”。

截至2012年清明节，天津有据可查的遗体捐献者已有355人，将近三分之一是赵永华经手的。

他记得很清楚，2002年3月31日那天，他和妻子孙秀兰办完无偿捐献遗体的法律手续后就在自家门口钉了一个牌子——“天津市遗体捐献志愿者小组”，他们的家庭电话成了“捐献热线”。

起初，赵永华有点不乐意走进阴暗的解剖楼，“放死人的地方——（要是）放元宝的地方咱可以开开眼！”现在，半夜进去他也毫不怯场。

有一年除夕，他是在天津市河北区一家殡仪馆的太平间里度过的。那个夜晚的气氛让他想起了《聊斋志异》里“画皮”之类的鬼故事。当时，4个活人守着11个死人。殡仪馆的看门人喝起了酒，窗外烟花爆竹好不热闹。

下岗前的天津市机械链条厂经营科科长赵永华不知道什么是“遗体捐献”，这还是1998年妻子孙秀兰从报上学到的字眼。她对丈夫说：“捐了遗体，多省事儿啊！给孩子们省了大事儿了。”

赵永华感到奇怪：“妇科检查你都不乐意去，怎么遗体捐献你反而带了头了？”

一对儿女则激烈反对——“你们死了不管了，大爷、舅舅们会说我们把爸爸妈妈捐献了、大卸八块了太不孝顺。”

4年以后，子女才答应在他们的遗体捐

献申请表上签字。

他们没法不同意——父母已经干了不少“傻”事。

赵永华夫妇1993年成为志愿者。那一年，48岁的赵永华下岗回家。不久之后，孙秀兰厂内退休，月收入420元，养活一家六口。

但他们拒绝申请居民最低生活保障金。赵永华宁可每天出门去捡饮料瓶卖钱。为了省钱，夫妻二人相互理发。

“我们是工人，能拉得下脸来。”赵永华说。

在这种窘境下，他们还将自家电话设为“家庭扶老帮办热线”，尽量帮助弱势老人。

拨通这条热线的，“什么人都有”。最早本社区较多，如今连山西、内蒙、河北等外地也有。外地有位老干部退休后门可罗雀，感到孤独，时常打来电话聊天。

这些年里，赵永华夫妇还赡养了11位无依无靠的老人，并为其中的5位送了终。

起初，他把老人接到自己家住，但房子太小，他就出钱把老人送到养老院。

还有一对小两口儿上门来请赵永华给家里老人“做工作”，这一家四口人住在100多平方米的房子里，嫌挤，摩擦不断。

小两口儿原本以为热线电话的这边是个气派的政府调解部门，步入昏暗的墙皮剥落的楼道后，狐疑地问赵永华：“我们没走错吧？”

就跟上班一样，赵永华几乎每天早晨七点左右出门，从家里带好饭菜，骑车在天津转悠，一天少说要骑40公里，挨个看望老人。这些年，自行车他丢了几十辆。

他去老人院服务，不是像一些学生那样把老人叫醒，“奶奶你起来我给你唱个歌”，而是带着自己的孙女“看奶奶爷爷去”。每逢过年，他专找那些没人理睬、趴在窗户上看别人放爆竹的老人，把他们接到自己家里吃饺子。

赵永华做遗体捐献志愿者之后，老人们问他忙什么，他就顺便介绍一下。他说，以前遗体“让虫子给啃了、吃了”，现在送到医学院，“给孩子们做标本”，这个有价值。很多老人动了心。

不过，他从不在人们病危的时候跑去谈遗体捐献。那就“晚八春了”，他说。

他平时热心助老，像“走亲戚”一样交往，“人心换人心”，但坚决反对劝捐，因为中国几千年的传统是“入土为安”，“你去劝了，人家家里回头打起来了。你不能去劝人家，你只能跟人家说好处”。

谈到“好处”，他总是用浓重的天津卫口音强调：“大家都去买墓地，地底下都是洋灰坨子。咱们天津市喊着要建成大花园，你不重视这个，迟早就是个大墓地！”

有时，他会形容，人死了“这摊臭肉污染环境，遗体捐献是变废为宝”。

为了描述角膜移植如何给人带来光明，他伸出手指在人眼前晃来晃去：“十来分钟就移植上了，盲人就看见了，说‘五个手指头、四个手指头’，多好的事儿！”

虽然总是见证死别，但这么多年来，他从没为谁掉过眼泪。

接送死者后半夜独自回家的路上，赵永华会在心里琢磨：“挺好的一个人死了。”“最后我归结到一点——又一位高尚的人。”

他总觉得，捐献者就在天上看着自己，自己不能泄气，必须越做越好。“假如说真有下面，等将来我死了，对不起那些先走的，在那边见面了，人家说，‘老赵你骗了我’，‘老赵你也来了，我跟你谈谈心吧，这几年你不行啊，我们上当了’——我们别叫人埋怨。”

这些年来，他“耳朵里不好听的话都灌满了”。有亲戚说他们“有病”，嘲笑孙秀兰“黄瓜买弯的，西红柿买裂口的，辣子买黏糊的”。

孙秀兰格外俭省。她习惯去早市买前一天剩下的便宜菜。包顿饺子也要算计：白菜价贵的时候，包饺子一棵白菜3元钱，不如买一元钱5斤的胡萝卜，能吃两回。

这对夫妇近20年没置办过新衣。如今，他们全身几乎都是死者穿过的旧衣。家属们知道他们不忌讳，衣服、被褥一送就好几包。

他觉得，自己与这些捐献者生前是朋友，生病时自己去照顾过，去世后自己亲手把他们送走，“分不开了”。

抬遗体的时候，这个1.65米的小个子

习惯扶着死者头部，那通常是长子的位置。他以此表达对死者的敬意。

赵永华只有一套新衣。他从国务院副总理手里领过“爱心捐助奖”。为了领奖，外甥女给他买了一套西装。从此一有应酬他就穿上，脏了也舍不得洗，衣服变得油亮油亮的。妻子开玩笑说：“下雨出去穿，正好当雨衣。”

老赵家的宝贝全在卧室。那里并排存着大约40个文件夹，里面是他这些年做的各类事情的记录，譬如：帮谁取了汇款，给谁买了尿不湿；62岁孤独老人在电话里托他帮忙找个伴儿，“男女都可”；有意捐献的人又来电话说，“儿子不同意捐”；甚至有自称忙于生意的陌生人希望通过老赵找人帮忙“搞家里卫生”。

只有小学文凭的赵永华写字极为工整，尽管里面别字不少，诸如“取缔”写成“去蹄”。

他的脾气并不像他的笔迹那样圆润。常年跟红十字会、公证处、医科大学等许多单位打交道，他摔过领导的电话，批评过“要不你们别坐这椅子上”。为了给遗体捐献者免除公证费，他“串门一样”天天去争取。这项200元的费用免了以后，他像打了胜仗一般兴奋。

多数时候，老赵和和气气地跟这些部门打交道。“他们态度好不好跟我没嘛关系——我就拿他们当一部机器。”

这个小学毕业生曾应邀去大学里给学生讲课，讲生命的意义。他被学生们尊称“赵老师”。

天津市发展和改革委员会就五年规划向公众征集建议，290多条整理成册的建议中，署名“赵永华”的有7条。在他看来，这是“玩儿”，也是尽“公民的责任”。他热心很多公益事，有一次，手术没多久的他插着尿管、把尿袋缝在裤子里去参加活动。

不进祖坟的决定，赵永华还没告诉河北省沧州市吴桥县老家的亲戚们。他说，不知情的亲戚也许会以为他在哪儿“被枪毙了”，回不来了。

对于儿孙，他表示“没嘛可留的”。眼下，他教孙女每天捐一块钱，“养成一种生活习惯”。包括他在内，每个家庭成员都有自己的捐款计划。

他知道自己将被解剖，什么都不会留下。天长日久泡着药水，皮肤会从浅黄变成深褐色。他还听说，自己的胳膊也许会跟别人的腿混在一起，难分彼此。

赵永华心平气和地等待那一天的来临，“我就乐乐呵呵，今天我起来了，我就干，明天人家没看见我，说老赵怎么没来呢——死啦！”

The Last Presents of Life

Over the past decade, Zhao Yonghua, a worker who had been laid off, has sent off one deceased person per month on average. He always brought a white flower with him so he could have it whenever needed.

The 67-year-old had carried 116 bodies onto the vans and sent them to the Anatomy Building of Tianjin Medical University. He was keenly aware that someday he too will be carried into that gray building and become the target of the students' scalpels, and people will wear the same flower on their chests to bid him farewell. At that time, his corneas will be removed first to save two blind people. Zhao opened one of his eyes wide with his fingers and said, "One person for two people."

Up until Qingming Festival in 2012, the number of registered body donors in Tianjin had amounted to 355, nearly one third of them were handled by Zhao.

He remembered clearly that on March 31, 2002, he and his wife, Sun Xiulan, nailed a plate outside their doorstep after completing their body donation legal procedures, which read "Body Donation Volunteer Group of Tianjin." Their home telephone thus became a "donation hotline."

In the very beginning, Zhao was reluctant to walk into that gloomy anatomy building. "It's where the dead bodies are placed — I may want to go if this place had gold ingots!" But now, he does not have any fear at all, even when entering at midnight.

He spent one Spring Festival Eve at the mortuary of a funeral parlor in Hebei District, Tianjin. The atmosphere that night had reminded him of the ghost stories in *Strange Stories from a Chinese Studio*, a collection of supernatural tales written at the turn of the 18th century. There were four of them staying with 11 deceased individuals. The doorkeeper began drinking alcohol, as many fireworks were lit outside to usher in the lunar New Year.

Before becoming laid-off, Zhao Yonghua served as a section chief at the Tianjin Mechanical Chain Factory. Back then, he had never heard of body donation. In 1998, his wife learned of this by reading the newspaper and said to him, "Donating our bodies can save a lot of trouble for our children!"

Zhao was surprised and asked her, "You're scared to even go to gynecological examinations, why are you so willing to donate your body?"

Their son and daughter expressed strong opposition to this, and said, "If you donate your bodies, all of our relatives will blame us for not being filial to our parents!"

It was not until four years later did the two agree to sign on the body donation application form for the older couple.

They had to do so, because their parents had done many "foolish" things.

Zhao and his wife became volunteers in 1993. It was also that year when the 48-year-old lost his job. Not long after that, his wife Sun was forced into an early retirement and had to provide for the whole family with her monthly income of 420 yuan.

However, they declined to apply for the minimum living allowance, and Zhao would rather go outside to pick up empty beverage bottles to make a living. To save money, the couple usually cut each other's hair.

"We are workers, and are scared to lose face," Zhao said.

Under such a predicament they still decided to set their phone number as the hotline to help the disadvantaged elderly.

A lot of people had called the number for a variety of reasons. When it was first opened, most of the calls they received were from their community. Now, people from places across the country, such as Shanxi, Inner Mongolia, and Hebei, also call them for help. A non-local older official feels very lonely after retirement, so he often calls to chat with the couple.

Over the years, Zhao and Sun have been supporting 11 seniors in need and sent five of them off as they passed away.

At first, Zhao let them live in his home. But as the house was too small to accommodate so many people, he paid to send them off to nursing homes.

A young couple came to Zhao and asked him to persuade their parents. Living in an apartment of over 100 square meters, the four members of their family felt it was too crowded and often argued with each other.

The callers used to think that the other side of the hotline was a government mediation department. After stepping into the dark and shabby corridor, they suspiciously asked Zhao, "Are we going the wrong way?"

Zhao Yonghua usually left home around 7 o'clock every morning with a meal that had been prepared to last the entire day. Every day, he would ride his bicycle at least 40 kilometers to visit the elderly living across the city. He had lost dozens of bikes over the years.

When serving the elderly in the nursing home, Zhao often brought his granddaughter and told her to "just visit the grandpas and grandmas" instead of waking them up by saying, "Grandma, let me sing a song for you." Every Spring Festival, he would bring the lonely seniors to his home to enjoy dumplings together.

After becoming a body donation volunteer, Zhao was often asked by the elderly what he had been busy with. He would make some introduction to them by saying, "In the past, after people passed away, their bodies might be eaten by worms in the ground; now, they are sent to the medical colleges and become samples for the students, so they can have a worthy death." Many old people were touched by the idea.

However, he had never discussed the topic when the patient was critically ill. According to him, that would be "too late."

Although having been treating the seniors like family, Zhao was strongly against the act of persuading them to donate their bodies because the Chinese tradition of laying someone to rest underground has been held for several thousand years. "If you try to persuade them, conflicts may occur among their family members. So instead of asking them to do so, you should only tell them about its benefits."

Speaking of the "benefits" of body donation, Zhao always stressed in his strong Tianjin accent, "If all residents try to buy a cemetery plot for themselves, there will be countless cement lumps underground. We have vowed to build Tianjin into a great garden, but if we don't pay attention to this, our city would become a giant graveyard sooner or later!"

Sometimes, he made such a description, "Rather than letting the body contaminate the environment, why not turn it into a treasure through body donation?"

When describing to others how corneal transplants can restore vision, he spread his fingers in front of their eyes and said, "It only takes ten minutes or so to complete the surgery, and then the blind patient may tell you, 'I can see five fingers now…' Isn't that amazing?"

Having witnessed death on so many occasions, Zhao had never shed tears for anyone over the years.

On his way back home at night after sending off the deceased, he often thought, "Such a good person has left this world. I made the conclusion in the end — another person with a noble character."

He always feels that the donors are watching him from Heaven, so he should never be discouraged by hardships and must make more progress in this endeavor. "If the afterlife really exists and I didn't work hard, I don't know how I can face those who passed away before me.

When we meet there, they may say to me, 'You cheated me, Lao Zhao', or 'You also came, Lao Zhao. I want to have a talk with you. You've been doing so badly in recent years, and all of us were taken in.'— I should not make them complain."

Over the years, his ears had been flooded with sarcastic remarks and complaints. Some relatives said they were "crazy" and mocked Sun Xiulan as a stingy housewife as she bought "crooked cucumbers, tomatoes with cracks, and stale chilies."

Having been living a frugal life, Sun often went to the morning market to buy the cheap vegetables from the day before. She is even thrifty when making dumplings: when the price of Chinese cabbage is high, each one might cost three yuan, so it would be better to eat carrots, which are 0.4 yuan per kilo.

The couple hasn't purchased any new clothing for themselves over the past two decades. Now, they often wear the old clothes of the deceased individual whose family knew that they never saw it as a taboo and often sent them plenty of clothes and beddings.

To Zhao, the donors were all his friends when they were alive, he took care of them when they were ill, and he sent them off after they passed away — he connected with them.

When carrying the dead bodies, Zhao, who is only 1.65 meters in height, often used his hand to support the head of the deceased, a task usually taken by the eldest son. He did this to show respect.

Zhao Yonghua only had one set of new clothing. He once received the "caring donors' award" from the Vice Premier of the State Council. To prepare for the grand event, his niece bought a set of Western suits for him. From then on, he would wear it on all important social occasions and was reluctant to wash it even if the clothes had become dirty. As time went by, it was covered with grease. His wife joked, "You can wear it as a raincoat!"

Zhao's bedroom was full of "treasures." Around 40 file folders were placed side by side. In them are the records of the things he had done over the years, such as the person's name whom he helped to draw remittance, and the one for whom he bought adult diapers; a 62-year-old senior called him asking for help in finding a partner; a potential donor made a phone call again telling him "My son won't allow me to do so"; a stranger even asked him to help find someone to clean his house because he was very busy with his business.

Zhao, who had only graduated from elementary school, has very neat handwriting despite some incorrectly written characters.

However, his temper is not as good as his handwriting. Having been in contact with the Red Cross Society, notary office, and medical colleges for so many years, he had scolded the leaders over the phone, saying they should not be idle in their positions. In order to exempt the body donors from notarial charges, he visited the notary office almost every day to get it done. Upon learning that the 200-yuan charge was removed, he became so excited as if he had won a crucial battle.

In most cases, he got along very well with these departments. "It doesn't matter to me whether they are friendly or not, I just take them as a machine."

He was invited to give lectures to college students on such topics as the meaning of life and they addressed him respectfully as "Teacher Zhao."

The Tianjin Development and Reform Commission had solicited suggestions from the general public about the municipality's five-year plan. Among the more than 290 pieces of advice which had been classified into volumes, seven carried the signature of Zhao Yonghua. Though he had no high hopes that they could become reality someday, he believed he was doing this to perform his civic responsibilities. As an active participant in various public welfare undertakings, he once attended an event with a catheter and a urine bag sewn into his trousers not long after a surgery.

Zhao had not yet told his relatives in their hometown of Wuqiao County, Cangzhou, Hebei Province of his decision not to be buried in their ancestral graveyard. He was afraid that those who didn't know the real situation might think he was "executed by shooting" somewhere and could never go back.

Zhao had said he has nothing to leave to his descendants. Now he requires his granddaughter to donate one yuan each day so that she can "form a good life habit." Every member of the family, including him, has their own donation plans.

He knew that his body will be dissected and nothing would be left. As time goes by, his skin color will turn brown from yellow in formalin. Someone also told him that his arms may be put together with another person's legs.

Zhao Yonghua has been waiting calmly for that day to come, "I just keep a positive mood every day. Today, I get up and do my work, and if you don't see me tomorrow and wonder why 'Lao Zhao' hasn't shown up, I may have already passed away!"

出版策划：王君校　韩　晖
统筹协调：付　眉　韩　颖　彭　博
策划编辑：刘小琳
责任编辑：陆　瑜
英文编辑：韩芙芸
封面设计：袁长新
排　　版：北京几何创想艺术设计有限公司
印刷监制：汪　洋

图书在版编目（CIP）数据

志愿者：让爱传递到每个角落：汉英对照 / "最美中国人"丛书编委会编著. — 北京：华语教学出版社，2022.5
（最美中国人）
ISBN 978-7-5138-2278-7

Ⅰ. ①志… Ⅱ. ①最… Ⅲ. ①人物—先进事迹—中国—现代—汉、英 Ⅳ. ① K820.7

中国版本图书馆 CIP 数据核字 (2022) 第 044703 号

志愿者：让爱传递到每个角落

"最美中国人"丛书编委会 编著

*

华语教学出版社有限责任公司出版
（中国北京百万庄大街 24 号　邮政编码 100037）
电话：(86)10-68320585, 68997826
传真：(86)10-68997826, 68326333
网址：www.sinolingua.com.cn
电子信箱：hyjx@sinolingua.com.cn
北京虎彩文化传播有限公司印刷
2022 年（16 开）第 1 版
2022 年第 1 版第 1 次印刷
（汉英）
ISBN 978-7-5138-2278-7
006900